W9-AEG-463

THE LIBRARY OF
AMERICAN
LIVES AND TIMES™

# WYATT EARP

## The O.K. Corral and the
## Law of the American West

**William Urban**

The Rosen Publishing Group's
PowerPlus Books™
New York

*Dedicated to Ilsabe, Elke, and Karl*
*for still considering Central Kansas home*
*even though they grew up in Wyatt Earp's birthplace*

Published in 2003 by The Rosen Publishing Group, Inc.
29 East 21st Street, New York, NY 10010

First Edition

*Editor's Note: All quotations have been reproduced as they appeared in
the letters and diaries from which they were borrowed. No correction was
made to the inconsistent spelling that was common in that time period.*

O.K. Corral is trademarked by Tombstone Historama Corporation, Tombstone, AZ

**Library of Congress Cataloging-in-Publication Data**

Urban, William L., 1939–
    Wyatt Earp : the O.K. Corral and the law of the American
West / by William L. Urban.
       p. cm. — (The library of American lives and times)
    Includes bibliographical references and index.
    Contents: America moves west — The Earp Family — Wyatt
grows up — Wyatt becomes a lawman — Tombstone — The gunfight
at the O.K. Corral — The vendetta ride — Wyatt's golden years — The
legacy of Wyatt Earp.
    ISBN 0-8239-5740-3
    1. Earp, Wyatt, 1848–1929—Juvenile literature   2. Peace offi-
cers—Southwest, New—Biography—Juvenile literature   3. United
States marshals—Southwest, New—Biography—Juvenile literature
4. Tombstone (Ariz.)—History—Juvenile literature   5. Violence—
Arizona—Tombstone—History—19th century—Juvenile literature
6. Southwest, New—Biography—Juvenile literature  [1. Earp, Wyatt,
1848–1929  2. Peace officers  3. Tombstone (Ariz.)—History  4.
Violence  5. Frontier and pioneer life—Southwest, New]  I. Title
II. Series
    F786.E18 U73  2002                  2001-005540
    978'.02'092—dc21
    [B]

Manufactured in the United States of America

# CONTENTS

1. America Moves West . . . . . . . . . . . . . . . . . .5

2. The Earp Family . . . . . . . . . . . . . . . . .14

3. Wyatt Grows Up . . . . . . . . . . . . . . . . .31

4. Wyatt Becomes a Lawman . . . . . . . . . . . . . .43

5. Tombstone . . . . . . . . . . . . . . . . . . .54

6. The Gunfight at the O.K. Corral . . . . . . . . . . .66

7. The Vendetta Ride . . . . . . . . . . . . . . . .80

8. Wyatt's Golden Years . . . . . . . . . . . . . . .86

9. The Legacy of Wyatt Earp . . . . . . . . . . . . .94

   Timeline . . . . . . . . . . . . . . . . . . .100
   Glossary . . . . . . . . . . . . . . . . . . .103
   Additional Resources . . . . . . . . . . . . . .107
   Bibliography . . . . . . . . . . . . . . . . .108
   Index . . . . . . . . . . . . . . . . . . . .109

# 1. America Moves West

You might have heard of the O.K. Corral and Wyatt Earp. You certainly have an image of what it was like to live in the Wild West from the countless movies and television programs that have focused on this part of America's history. The Wild West evokes images of lawless men and gunfights, and of towns full of men who would sooner shoot you than look at you. In some cases, these images might have been real. As settlers headed west and towns sprang up, the growth in population was huge. It was so great, in fact, that people got to the West before a system of laws did. This produced a situation in which men who had character and determination could succeed, but in which people who wanted to take advantage of the lack of law enforcement in less honorable ways could easily do so. It fell to some men to try to impose order on people who had come west for their own reasons. Wyatt Earp was one of these men. He upheld the law among cowboys,

*Opposite*: Wyatt Earp was considered a good-looking man. This photo, the most famous one taken of Wyatt, is from about 1887, six years after the gunfight at the O.K. Corral. It was taken while he was in the San Diego area.

prospectors, and settlers, not all of whom saw eye to eye. He relied on honor, the code of the West, to guide his actions. The story of Wyatt Earp is in essence the story of the West and a unique period in America's history. The story begins years before Wyatt Earp was even born.

● ● ● ● ● ●

American colonists had huddled along the Atlantic coast for most of the seventeenth and eighteenth centuries, finding safety and financial success in the growing cities of New England. The land along the frontier, west of the Appalachian Mountains, was, in contrast, unsafe and uninviting. The French had supported Indian attacks on British colonists and their isolated homes and communities west of the Appalachians throughout the French and Indian War (1754–1763) and the British then forbade the colonists from crossing the Appalachian Mountains and settling the vast Midwest. It was only after the American Revolution (1775–1783) that the first American pioneers began to enter what are now Tennessee and Kentucky. In the War of 1812, several leading Indian nations made one last effort to drive back these newcomers, but they lacked the numbers, the organization, and the technology needed to succeed. By 1815, the Americans had opened the way to the West.

---

*Opposite:* The United States looked quite different in 1816 from how it looks today. Much of what is now part of the United States was still unexplored frontier, or territory belonging to European nations such as Britain and Spain, as shown in this 1816 map entitled *Map of the United States with the Contiguous British & Spanish Possessions.*

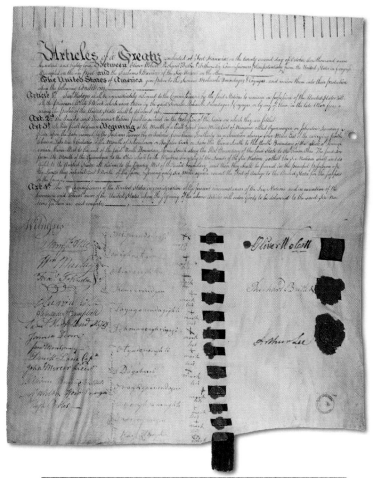

In treaties such as this one signed with the Six Nations at Fort Stanwix in 1784, Indians gave up their eastern lands. As Americans moved into traditional hunting and gathering grounds, Indians could no longer find enough food, and diseases from contact with Americans were destroying them. Many Indians thought it was better to move west and to be taught agriculture and other new skills that would enable them to prosper. These plans did not always work out.

American settlers poured out of the east in covered wagons, on rafts, and on foot.

Largely unpopulated lands filled first with farms, then with small towns, and finally with cities. For centuries Native Americans had migrated over this vast territory.

Although a few tribes managed to retain some of their ancestral lands, most signed away their rights in peace treaties and then moved farther west, away from the new settlers. Although Americans acknowledged the Native American heritage by retaining the native names for rivers and mountains, much of the Native American culture was lost. In their enthusiasm for new land, the new settlers in the West thought more about their own future than about the Native Americans' past.

Among the early pioneers who crossed the Appalachian Mountains was Walter Earp. He had come to Tennessee from North Carolina in 1813, then traveled

This painting of Daniel Boone by George Caleb Bingham was made from 1851 to 1852. Daniel Boone is leading pioneers through the Cumberland Gap in the Appalachians. Boone was responsible for the exploration and the settlement of Kentucky.

farther west to Kentucky in 1815. He was a school-teacher and, when trained clergy were not available, a preacher. He never earned much money, but by moving from community to community, he made enough to support his large family.

The Earps, like many pioneers, relied on their own efforts to provide religious services for their community. The Earps, who were Methodists, depended on special ministers called circuit riders, who visited small communities on a regular schedule, to provide religious services. Walter Earp was a deeply religious man who named several sons, including Nicholas Porter Earp, after these famous circuit riders. Nicholas was to be the father of Wyatt Earp.

Religion was not the only area in which American pioneers had to learn to take care of themselves. They assisted one another in clearing the land of trees, in barn raising, in bringing in the autumn harvest, in preserving food, and even in hunting. Neighbors learned to work together, strengthening the already existing concepts of democracy. This spirit of practical cooperation, in fact, is often thought to be one of the most important characteristics of the American settlers. In learning to take care of themselves, however, Americans also developed a sense of individualism that ran contrary to the spirit of cooperation. Moreover, this spirit of individualism was sometimes completely opposed to traditional concepts of law and order. There was a restless energy to conquer new lands and to make new fortunes. Settlers would often bend and break the law in order to get ahead.

By the late 1820s, the restless energy of Americans drove them into new fields of activity. They cleared woods for farming, started businesses, and transported wood and agricultural products down the Ohio and Mississippi Rivers. Although some Americans were willing to work for wages until they had a stake or sufficient money and personal possessions to strike out on their own, many were so desperate for farms of their own that they moved west and squatted on unclaimed or unoccupied land. The westward movement of this generation happened faster than anyone had anticipated. One result was that the institutions of government lagged behind the furious pace of settlement. When confronting danger, with no laws for protection and no sheriffs or police forces, individuals often reached for knives or dueling pistols to protect themselves. Perhaps almost as often, it was a person's personal honor rather than physical safety that was challenged. A stain on someone's honor could be washed away only by a humble apology or by blood.

This combination of energy, ambition, and sense of honor would be seen in the career of Wyatt Earp. It would be seen both in his character and in his actions, and it would motivate the men who either loved or hated him. The men who met in the street in Tombstone, Arizona, on October 26, 1881, and squared

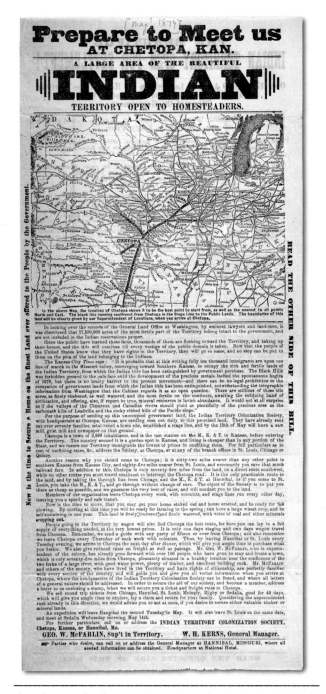

People who read advertisements, such as this one published
in 1879, were enticed by the idea of cheap, unsettled land.
The ad reads, "Prepare to meet us at Chetopa, Kan. a large area
of the beautiful Indian Territory open to homesteaders."

off in deadly combat at the O.K. Corral had a lot in common. They understood one another very well.

The Earps' story summarizes much of what was true of America in this era. The facts are few, partly because society was still too primitive and poor to write them down, but also because this was a time of rapid change. The Earps were among the first families to cross the mountains. They cleared land and built forts to protect their families against Indian attack. They learned that to survive on the frontier you had to rely on family, friends, and most of all yourself, and they moved farther west at the first opportunity. Ambitious and optimistic, the Earps were typical pioneers.

# 2. The Earp Family

Nicholas Earp's first wife died in 1839. About one year later, Nicholas married Virginia Ann Cooksey. He or his brother Lorenzo may have visited Illinois in 1843, but it was two years later that they took their families to western Illinois. In 1845, when Nicholas and Virginia Earp came to Monmouth, Illinois, the town consisted of a few hundred people living around the courthouse square. The rolling, tall grass prairie that began a few blocks away was cut by numerous creeks and was dotted with patches of woods. The Pioneer Cemetery, where the Earps buried their dead, was outside town. Today it is near the center of the city of Monmouth, and only a handful of the worn tombstones from the frontier days can be read. There were a couple of hotels, a stagecoach stop, a few stores, a poorly made jail, and a courthouse. Churches and schools were makeshift operations. Nicholas either bought or built a small house one block northeast of the square for his wife, his three boys, and his newborn daughter.

Walter and Martha Earp brought the rest of the family, about forty in number, to Monmouth in November 1846. Walter, already at an appropriate age to retire, ran for the office of justice of the peace the next year. This was a minor position that required no judicial training, but it provided him with a small income and the title of judge.

The Earp clan was one of the largest families in the small community. We can say "clan" because the Earps were a close-knit family, with obvious love and affection for one another, especially for Martha. Each of the various families within the clan had a child every two years or so, which meant that their small, rented houses quickly filled to capacity. Privacy and comfort were not a part of daily life. Entertainment was homemade and usually involved telling stories, making conversation, and indulging in a lot of local gossip. The Earp men were good citizens. They were hardworking churchgoers, and, with few exceptions, they were strongly opposed to drinking alcohol. They were solidly working class, with limited resources to buy land and the expensive equipment that was necessary to break the prairie sod, work the soil, and harvest the crops, but they were proud of the moderate success that they enjoyed. Within a few years of arriving in Monmouth, Illinois, they were almost all able to purchase homes.

One exception was Wyatt's father, Nicholas. He was unhappy with the low wages he earned as a cooper,

making barrels for the region's animal and agricultural products. Monmouth's deep black soil and dependable rainfall almost guaranteed good crops of wheat and corn. However, there seemed to be no way for Nicholas to get his hands on any of this incredibly rich farmland. Monmouth lay in the military tract. The government had surveyed the land between the Illinois and Mississippi Rivers and had given 40-acre (16.2-ha) parcels suitable for farming to veterans of the American Revolution and the War of 1812. Despite having ancestors who would have qualified for a land grant, none of the living Earps did. Nicholas had to find some other way to make his fortune. He had observed his father's success as a justice of the peace and could imagine a similar career for himself, perhaps in an even higher office, but first he had to distinguish himself in some way to be a candidate for election. He was well liked in town, but that alone was unlikely to impress the lawyers and the clergymen who made up the Monmouth elite. Farmers judged a man by the yield of his fields and the size of his barns. In short, Nicholas saw no way to demonstrate his skills and value to the community. Moreover, he lost his temper when anyone questioned his competence or his judgment.

Nicholas Earp saw the Mexican War as the perfect opportunity to acquire both fame and a farm. In 1847, he

---

Opposite: Nicholas and Virginia Earp were married on July 30, 1840. Nicholas was 26 years old. This photo was taken later in their lives, after much of their family was grown.

In 1847, Nicholas Earp joined the Monmouth Dragoons and escorted military supply trains out of Veracruz during the Mexican War. This print, entitled *Scene in Veracruz During the Bombardment, March 25, 1847*, shows a scene from a battle there. The print was created in New York by E. B. & E. C. Kellogg in 1847.

*The Mexican War resulted from what Americans called Manifest Destiny, meaning that it was obvious that nothing would stop American pioneers from reaching the Pacific Ocean. Mexico suffered from political and economic instability. As Americans moved west, they saw a vast land claimed by Mexico but very lightly populated. Most of the mountains and the deserts were inhabited only by a relatively small number of Native Americans and Mormons. Mexican refusal to recognize Texan independence was the most important issue, but trade across the Santa Fe Trail, the fur trade, and access to California were important, too. Mexicans, who see the causes of the war differently, refer to it as the War of American Aggression.*

volunteered for the Monmouth Dragoons and was named third sergeant. Despite a lack of training, this small cavalry unit was soon in Mexico, where they escorted military supply trains from Veracruz to Jalapa. There were few chances to demonstrate military valor, however, because whenever Mexican guerrillas were spotted, Texas Rangers went into battle, leaving the Illinois cavalry to guard the wagons. The Rangers were armed with the newly invented Colt revolver, and the Dragoons lacked combat experience. When fever and disease struck down many of his friends, Nicholas Earp accompanied them home. He had been temporarily disabled himself

This is a Colt Single Action Army revolver from 1883, that was owned by Wyatt Earp. A man named Samuel Colt invented the first practical revolver in 1836. This weapon would change the way wars were fought. Westerners were fond of saying, "God did not make all men equal, Colonel Colt did." Colt's guns were made in Hartford, Connecticut, but they found their biggest market in the West.

Texas Rangers, such as the one depicted in this 1848 wood engraving,
played a vital role in the Mexican War. This illustration was published
in John Frost's 1848 *Pictorial History of Mexico and the Mexican War*.
Stephen F. Austin formed the Texas Rangers in 1823 to protect his new
colony. He wrote that he would "employ ten men. . .to act as rangers
for the common defense." The group was enlarged in 1835 to protect
the colony as tensions over Texas independence grew.

and was sent home for good after being kicked in the groin by a mule. He returned to Monmouth only days before the birth of a son, whom he named in honor of his commanding officer, Wyatt Berry Stapp. On the day Wyatt Berry Stapp Earp was born, March 19, 1848, there was said to have been a light snowfall.

Nicholas's hopes of obtaining a farm vanished when the U.S. government announced that there would be no land grants to veterans of the Mexican War. Nicholas was heartbroken. His family continued to struggle with poverty, and he was desperate to find a way to care for them. In 1849, Nicholas decided that he would travel to California to make his fortune. He sold his home, packed up his family, and started west. However, he did not get farther west than Pella, Iowa, about 150 miles (241 km) from Monmouth. It is not clear why he changed his mind. It might have been that news had come back overland that the gold rush of 1848 was finished. It might have been family considerations, or it might have been the beautiful fields of central Iowa. He bought a house in Pella and prospered as a farmer in this very moral, hardworking, Dutch community.

In 1856, when Wyatt was eight years old, the Earps moved back to Monmouth. Their reasons for doing so are not clear. Dutch-speaking children had filled the public schools in Pella, making it difficult for Wyatt and his siblings to understand their lessons. Even the local newspaper was written in Dutch, so Nicholas might have missed

While in Pella, the Earps lived in the Van Spankeren House, at 507 E. Franklin Street. The home, built around 1850, is now a museum and part of the Pella, Iowa, Historical Village.

the English-speaking environment of home. He had certainly heard that the Monmouth economy had boomed after the railroad arrived. Perhaps he also felt an obligation to care for his mother, who had been widowed three years before. He had enough money to buy a house, but not enough to buy a farm. Most likely Nicholas was more interested in politics than in farming, anyway. He was among the founders of the Republican Party in Warren County and led the cheers for John Charles Frémont, the western explorer who was the party's first presidential candidate in 1856. Nicholas was soon elected constable. This job mainly involved delivering summons and collecting fines. However, riding around town on official business allowed Nicholas and his brother Walter to open a profitable business on the side. They began bootlegging whiskey in Monmouth, which was a dry community. This was a very illegal activity.

Nicholas's liquor business eventually attracted the attention of the Monmouth College president, both town newspaper editors, and several local clergymen. In 1859, after being convicted and fined three times for selling whiskey, Nicholas angrily sold his property and moved back to Pella.

The Monmouth years had been important for

A famous explorer during America's westward expansion, John C. Frémont earned the nickname the Pathfinder. In 1856, Frémont unsuccessfully campaigned for president. Even his father-in-law publicly sided against him. His campaign ribbon is pictured above.

REFERENCES.
1. COURT HOUSE
2. COUNTY JAIL
3. MONMOUTH COLLEGE
4. ACADEMY
5. NORTH
6. EAST } PUBLIC SCHOOL
7. SOUTH
8. WEST
9. C.B.& Q. R.R. DEPOT
10. T.P.& W. DEPOT
11. GAS WORKS
12. HAMILTON PHOTOGRAPH GALLERY
13. COLONEL SCHOOL

BIRD'S EYE
MON
WARREN COUNT

MONMOUTH COLLEGE.

DRAWN BY A. RUGER.

OF THE CITY OF

UTH.

ILLINOIS 1869.

TH WEST.

CHURCHES.
12. BAPTIST.
13. CHRISTIAN
14. METHODIST
15. 1ST PRESBYTERIAN
16. 2D
18. 3D PRESBYTERIAN
19. R. CATHOLIC

ACADEMY.

MERCHANT'S LITHOGRAPHING CO. CHICAGO.

young Wyatt, who probably heard Abraham Lincoln speak only a couple of blocks from his home, who grew up in often crippling poverty, who saw his father perform both legal and illegal jobs, and who came to sympathize with his father's rants about his many enemies. Wyatt learned attitudes that formed the foundation of his character. He learned about the importance of family and the need to stand up for what he believed, even when the belief was unpopular. He also came to understand that law on the American frontier was more complicated than it seemed. Some people believed drinking liquor and gambling could be tolerated among those who wouldn't abuse the privileges, but that laws had to be enforced against those who lacked self-control. Others insisted on the strict enforcement of all laws for all people. Wyatt admired his father, but he also learned from his father's mistakes. Wyatt saw that success depended on having the right friends, especially newspaper editors and churchmen. Throughout his life, Wyatt cultivated friendships with such influential men. Furthermore, he learned the importance of curbing his temper. To the world, Wyatt Earp wanted to give the impression that he was cool, calm, and capable. This was easier to say than to do, because Wyatt was as

---

*Previous spread:* The Earps lived in Monmouth, shown in this 1869 bird's-eye view drawn by A. Ruger, until Nicholas was caught selling liquor illegally one too many times. Monmouth experienced economic growth with the arrival of a railroad in 1853. A new commercial center sprang up. It can be seen on this map, around the 500 and 600 blocks of South 3rd Street.

The legend on this 1874 Currier and Ives print reads, "Woman's Holy War. Grand charge on the Enemy's Works." It refers to the temperance and prohibition movements, which were advocated by many women. Here women with large battle-axes shatter barrels of beer, whiskey, gin, rum, and "Wine & Liquors."

In the early 1800s, Americans were consuming incredible amounts of alcoholic beverages. Excessive drinking resulted in workplace injuries, poor general health, and early deaths. Social reformers argued that most cases of poverty, child abuse, wife beating, gambling, and crime were associated with heavy drinking. When efforts to encourage moderate drinking, or the temperance movement, failed, reformers began working toward eliminating all forms of alcohol consumption. Protestant churches soon insisted that members avoid using alcohol and tobacco. As happened later during Prohibition (1919–1933), a time when drinking alcohol was outlawed, alcohol consumption went down, but many people found ways to buy liquor illegally. These individuals often lost respect for the government and the officers charged with enforcing an unpopular law.

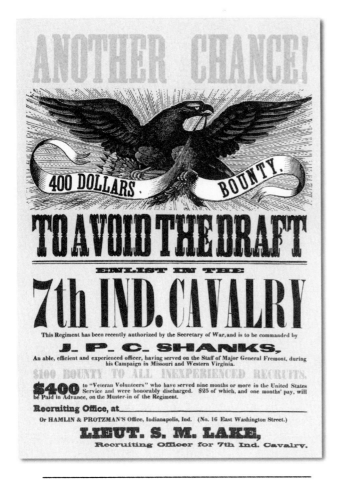

The Union needed to increase the size of their army during the Civil War, so they started a draft requiring all men between the ages of 20 and 45 to serve. Many people did not wish to serve so they paid a fee to have a substitute enroll in their place. This poster is advertising the chance to avoid the draft.

impulsive and hot-blooded as any other young man trying to become an adult.

Three of Wyatt's brothers served in the Union army during the Civil War (1861–1865). Newton joined an Iowa cavalry regiment, and Jim and Virgil Earp returned to Warren County in Illinois to fight beside their friends. All the Earps were patriots, and they shunned friends and relatives who chose to stay home and to earn good wages during the war years. Wyatt himself was too young to enlist, but he later said he tried to run away to join the army, only to be caught by his father. He also spoke of farming 80 acres (32 ha) single-handedly. Sometimes he said the land was in Iowa,

*The western tall tale was an art form in which the soft-spoken Wyatt excelled. It was considered very funny to pull the legs of "tenderfeet," easterners, who listened openmouthed to far-fetched stories. Eastern humor was based on wit and clever wordplay, but western humor lay in the way the story was told, often using colorful western slang. We have few examples of Wyatt's exact words, which lay buried underneath lawyers' briefs, reporters' exaggerations, and friends' lack of writing talent, but we know some of the practical jokes that he played on newcomers to Dodge City. He was a very sober man who rarely laughed or smiled in public, but in the West that was no sign a man lacked a sense of humor.*

sometimes he said it was in Illinois. In any case, it is an unlikely story, one of Wyatt's western tall tales, but one probably rooted in the memory of hard labor in those days.

Wyatt grew tall and sturdy during the war. As a grown man, he was a little more than 6 feet (2 m) tall and muscular. Because men were much shorter in those days, and because medical treatment could not correct many birth defects and injuries, Wyatt would have been considered a much more impressive figure than he might seem today. As he reflected on his situation, he saw that he had missed the excitement of the Civil War, that life on the Iowa frontier promised nothing more interesting than hoeing weeds in hot weather, and that talk about the weather did not satisfy the soul. Wyatt was eager to get out into the world.

# 3. Wyatt Grows Up

In 1864, Nicholas Earp led a wagon train to California, perhaps urged to immigrate there by a nephew who had settled there five years earlier. This was undoubtedly an exciting event for sixteen-year-old Wyatt. Not only was the journey over the prairie and the mountains difficult, but the presence of Native Americans could prove dangerous. The 1862 Sioux attack on Minnesota had not been forgotten. It was an effort by the largest Native American tribe in the north to drive the new settlers back toward the east. The settlers retaliated with attacks on Native Americans that included the notorious 1864 massacre by Colorado miners at Sand Creek. The Earps, like the many others who traveled on the Oregon Trail that summer, must have been constantly on the alert for attack.

Once across the Sierra Nevada, Nicholas bought a ranch near Colton, California, not far from San Bernardino. While in Colton, Wyatt worked as a farmer and later as a teamster, driving wagons. In addition, he was probably required to help in his father's saloon. In

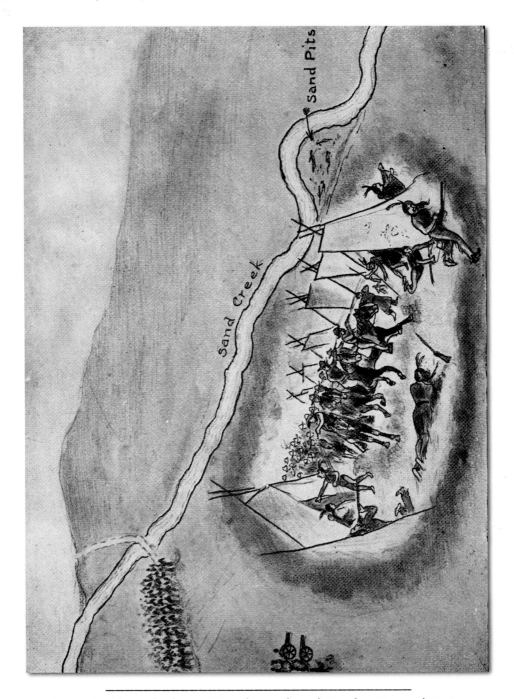

A drawing from the late 1800s shows the relative locations of Native American (Cheyenne) tepees and the members of the Third Colorado Regiment at the start of the battle at Sand Creek, Colorado.

*The Oregon Trail was the principal route west across the plains and mountains. As soon as the grass was up in spring, pioneers set out across Nebraska and Wyoming to Utah. Although some settlers turned northwest toward Oregon, the Earp party crossed the deserts of Nevada into the mountains of California, probably reaching Sacramento early in the fall.*

the summer of 1868, Nicholas went east to visit his mother, taking much of the family. When the family passed through Wyoming, Wyatt and Virgil apparently stayed behind to work as laborers on the railroad. When the outbreak of new Indian wars made it unsafe to recross the plains, Nicholas joined his brother Jonathan in Lamar, Missouri, near the Kansas border. There Nicholas took a variety of jobs, among them running a restaurant in a hotel, and he was elected justice of the peace.

When Wyatt joined his father in Lamar, Nicholas employed him as a waiter. Working at the hotel had one

A steam shovel works in Fish Cut, in Green River, Wyoming,
during construction work on the Union Pacific Railroad.
Wyatt Earp and his brother Virgil spent some time working
on the construction of the railroad through Wyoming in 1868.

advantage: He married the owner's daughter, Rilla Sutherland (the spelling that some historians use, Urilla or Willa, may be a misreading of the handwriting on the marriage certificate), on January 24, 1870. Presiding over the ceremony was Justice of the Peace Nicholas Earp. Finding a suitable job in a small town was apparently difficult. Wyatt took the low-paying position of constable in March 1870 and in November was formally elected to the position, defeating his brother Newton, 137 to 108. The duties of the constable were few. Only a few years before, western Missouri had been a battleground of the Civil War, then the haunt of former Confederates, such as the James Brothers and the Younger Brothers. By the time Wyatt came to town, however, Lamar was a peaceful little community. Citizens were less concerned about crime than whether or not pigs should be allowed to run free in the streets.

Wyatt's plans changed suddenly when Rilla died, perhaps of typhus. After her death, Wyatt and the Earp brothers had a fistfight with Rilla's brothers and their friends for reasons that are still unknown. Wyatt then stole a horse and fled to Arkansas. Eventually the charge of horse stealing was dropped, but by that time Wyatt was somewhere in Indian Territory, or what is today Oklahoma. In Indian Territory, Wyatt had various adventures, including buffalo hunting, an activity which, over time, reduced the once vast herds of buffalo

This bandit weekly, *The Jesse James Stories,* running 138 issues between 1901 and 1903, competed against Tousey's *James Boys Weekly.* Pictured is issue 113, published in 1903 by Street and Smith.

*Jesse and Frank James and the Younger Brothers were the most famous of many gangs that terrorized the frontier after the Civil War. Newspaper reporters and writers of western tales made these train and bank robbers into romantic heroes. The public demanded a regular supply of stories, which meant that writers had to find, or invent, a regular supply of heroes. Fortunately for the writers, there were many authentic, heroic figures available: Wild Bill Hickok, Buffalo Bill Cody, Kit Carson, and later, Wyatt Earp.*

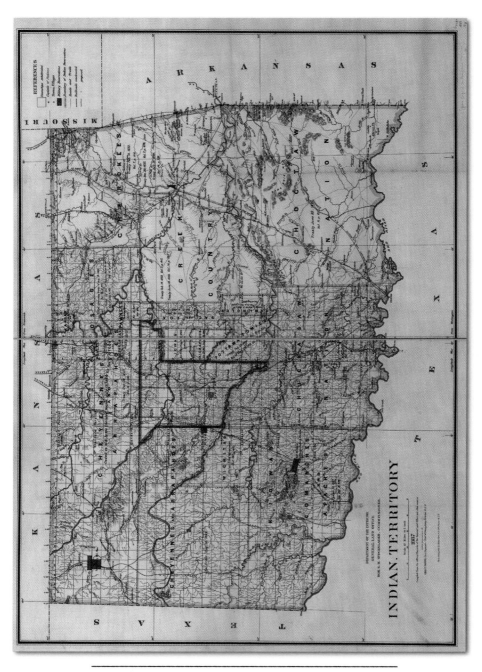

As Americans continued to settle in the West, the Native Americans were pushed out. The Indian Territory, today's Oklahoma, was land that was set aside for the transplanting of Indian tribes that were "in the way" of westward expansion. This 1887 map was compiled from the official records of the General Land Office and other sources under the supervision of George U. Mayo.

Bat Masterson was photographed in 1885, about the time he helped Doc Holliday avoid being brought back to Arizona from Colorado. Doc believed if he was brought back it would be his death warrant.

to near extinction. Wyatt met Bat Masterson in the area called Indian Territory in 1871. Bat would become Wyatt Earp's life-long friend and would share in many of Wyatt's adventures.

The area called Indian Territory was then about as wild a territory as any that existed. The Indian nations living there came from every corner of the United States. Thus they lacked unifying customs and languages. Organized government beyond the tribal level was represented by the territorial governor, a hand-ful of U.S. marshals, and the Indian agents. Chaos and disorganization, such as what existed in Indian Territory, always provided opportunities for both the very talented and the most unscrupulous people. Criminals flocked to

The frontier experience was more
complex than we might imagine.
The first Europeans or Americans to
enter new lands were usually
fur trappers, traders, and missionaries.
Prospectors came second, often followed
by hordes of miners. Next came the
cattlemen, and last the farmers. It might
sound like an orderly progression,
but often one wave would arrive hard
on the heels of those who had come earlier,
only to be overwhelmed by yet more
newcomers. In all, the settlement of the West
took less than a century. A Native American
who was a child when William Clark and
Meriwether Lewis made their expedition
in 1804 could have lived to witness the
last tribe confined to a reservation.

William Barclay "Bat" Masterson (1856-1921), one of the principal authors of the Wyatt Earp legend, later became a well-known sports-writer for a New York newspaper. Bat acquired a permanent limp in an 1876 gunfight, after which he carried a flashy cane. Once in Dodge City, when Wyatt was hauling a drunk off to jail by his ear, another cowboy drew a concealed weapon. Bat thumped the offender over the head with the cane, saving Wyatt's life.

Indian Territory in large numbers, to take advantage of the Native Americans or to evade arrest by lawmen from neighboring states. Bootleggers sold liquor in violation of tribal laws, lazy individuals wanted to be adopted into the tribes so they could qualify for the annual government sub-sidy, and outlaws wanted a hideout between robberies. There was also a large African American popula-tion. Some had been slaves of the Native Americans before the Emancipation Proclamation of January 1863; others had come west in search of freedom and better jobs. In this environ-ment, Wyatt Earp had ample opportunities to observe and to reflect on human character. When Wyatt came out of Indian Territory in 1873, he was

*Cattle towns existed to serve the cattle industry. Americans, with money earned during the post–Civil War prosperity, wanted meat on their tables. This provided jobs and livelihoods for many—for butchers, meat dealers, railroad construction workers, locomotive engineers, farmers who sold feed grain, and cowboys who drove the cattle north from Texas. It also provided prosperity for the newly founded railhead towns at the ends of the rail line. The cattle towns could prosper, however, only if they provided the market that the cattlemen wanted, the entertainment that the cowboys had dreamt about, and sufficient law enforcement to guarantee safety for the townspeople. The individual responsible for balancing these conflicting wishes was sometimes called a sheriff, sometimes a marshal, but whatever the title, the officer's job was a demanding one.*

no longer a wild and undisciplined boy. Wyatt Earp emerged a man.

Every summer during Wyatt's time in Indian Territory, cattlemen had been driving their herds from Texas to Kansas, following established routes to Abilene, Ellsworth, Wichita, and, later, Dodge City. These towns became famous, because they provided stockyards and loading facilities where the cattlemen could sell the animals and could pay the cowboys who had made the journey with them. The cowboys often celebrated at the end of a long period of hard work, then accompanied the cattle farther east or began the long ride back to Texas. Wyatt would eventually live in various cattle towns, hoping to strike it rich, but his great fortune would never come. Instead, he would find a career in law enforcement, trying to keep the rogue cowboys and other criminals from breaking the law.

# 4. Wyatt Becomes a Lawman

When Wyatt rode into Wichita, Kansas, in 1874, he was well prepared for the role of western legend. He was a healthy, good-looking young man with no obvious vices. At age twenty-six, he was experienced in handling horses and weapons. He had crossed the western frontier twice, had lived on the plains, and had worked with his hands. He was a good fistfighter, which was an advantage when he applied for a job as a policeman because the Wichita city council did not want policemen to shoot drunken cowboys. He had been a constable back in Lamar, Missouri, and was also a gambler who was familiar with the saloons of western cattle towns. He was moderate in eating and did not drink at all, traits that kept his figure trim. He was a Republican, and Kansas was largely a Republican state. Lastly, he was a man of few words in a culture that valued a man's ability to curb

*Next page*: Wyatt Earp traveled from town to town in the hopes of getting rich. He found work as a lawman in many of the towns in which he stopped. Wyatt Earp is pictured here in Dodge City, around 1883. Wyatt was a marshal there in the 1870s.

his tongue. Rarely did anyone make an enemy by remaining quiet when the opportunity presented itself to say something stupid.

In the cattle-driving years of the 1870s, Kansas was a meeting ground for southerners and northerners. The South was represented by Texas cowboys, some of whom were Confederate veterans of the Civil War, eager to have a good time after a long ride in cattle dust. The North was represented by cattle buyers, saloon keepers, farmers, merchants, church congregations, and military garrisons. Each railhead town needed policemen and sheriffs who sympathized with the North, but who would bend the law for the cowboys who played an important role in the cattle-based economy of the growing communities.

The moments of excitement were rare. Modern-day moviegoers might think that nothing happened in frontier towns except drinking, gambling, and fighting, but baseball games were common, as were cowboy bands, horse racing, and picnics. Public meetings, debates, and speeches were always well attended, and political intrigues seemed endless. One might easily find more drinking and fighting at a political rally than in a saloon. There was always courtroom drama, too. Most of the time, however, small-town life was dull. A dogfight might be the big public event of the day. Private life was more likely to center on conversation, courting, puffing on a pipe, speculating on the

*"Bleeding Kansas" was a familiar phrase
to anyone who lived in Illinois in the
late 1850s. Public opinion about slavery was
sharply divided, as demonstrated by the famous
1858 debates between Abraham Lincoln
and Stephen Douglas. Republicans believed
that Kansas should become a free state,
where slavery would be outlawed. Democrats
said that they believed in popular sovereignty,
meaning the right of local people to decide
what laws would apply locally. However,
when the citizens of Kansas territory appeared
ready to vote for a constitution that outlawed
slavery, Democrats in Missouri, a slave state,
decided to put a stop to it. They invaded
Kansas at election time to vote and to
intimidate those who might cast ballots
against slavery. In 1863, a small army
of Confederate raiders led by William
Quantrill burned Lawrence, the
largest town in Kansas, and killed
every male Jayhawker, as Kansans
called themselves, that they could find.*

weather, watching the neighbors, or thinking about tomorrow's work.

At some point after Rilla's death, Wyatt either married or began living with a woman named Mattie Blaylock. She was ten years younger than Wyatt and was born in Wisconsin. Almost nothing else is known about Mattie except that she was nice, dark haired, and rather boring. She was moderately good-looking, and she loved Wyatt. In contrast, Wyatt found her presence merely convenient. In frontier days, just as women could not do men's hard labor easily, a man working ten or more hours per day lacked the time and the energy for washing clothes and cooking. Wyatt liked clean shirts and modest, well-prepared meals, and Mattie

Wyatt Earp lived in Dodge City for about three years and worked as a lawman there. Front Street is pictured here in about 1879, the year that Wyatt Earp left for Tombstone, Arizona.

Celia Ann "Mattie" Blaylock Earp was Wyatt's wife or at least they lived together. Apparently their relationship was an unhappy one, as they broke up a few years after they arrived in Tombstone. This image is attributed to J. T. Parker and Company, Fort Scott, Kansas.

was a good partner to build a life with, even if Wyatt did not love her.

In 1876, Wyatt moved to Dodge City, Kansas, where he became deputy marshal. Wyatt shot only one man in Dodge City, a Texas cowboy who was riding up and down the main street at 3:00 A.M., shooting into the buildings. Wyatt was not even certain that he had fired the fatal shot, as he was not the only one eager to put a stop to the cowboy's actions. Most men buried in Boot Hill, the local cemetery, had died of illness rather than "with their boots on," a western phrase that meant you had been shot in a fight. Wyatt faced the additional danger of dealing constantly with armed men who lacked the stability provided by family responsibility. The lives of lawmen may have been boring and filled with trivial duties, but they were occasionally dangerous and short.

One of the ways for lawmen to protect themselves was to have loyal friends and deputies. Wyatt made a number of important friendships during his time as a lawman. One of the most important was with a man named John Henry "Doc" Holliday. Wyatt met Holliday in Texas in 1875, when Wyatt was a bounty hunter in

John Henry "Doc" Holliday, in this photograph from the early 1880s, was a dentist but seemed to spend most of his time playing cards and shooting people.

pursuit of a fugitive. Holliday was born in Georgia and was trained as a dentist (hence the "Doc") in Philadelphia. Dentistry was a good profession, because at the time almost everyone had bad teeth. However, Holliday suffered from a deadly lung disease called tuberculosis, which was common in the crowded, unsanitary living conditions of the age. In the early 1870s, he moved to Texas with the hope that the drier air would improve his health. There the tall, frail man began to drink heavily, a practice that somehow did not affect his ability to play cards well. Nor did it slow down his lightning draw in his many gunfights. The disease might have actually sharpened his already hot temper and led him to provoke enemies into offering deadly combat. This allowed him both to court death and to justify shooting others as self-defense. Doc Holliday became known as a dangerous man to cross, and by the time he reached Tombstone, almost everyone could recite a list of men Doc had gunned down. Newspapers and rumors exaggerated the number of men he had killed, making Doc into a mythic frontier figure in his own lifetime. A close bond formed between Wyatt and Doc. Perhaps it was because Wyatt ignored the danger of catching Doc's tuberculosis, which many others feared. Like most westerners, Wyatt was very loyal to his family and friends. There were few government services, and when situations arose that an individual could not handle alone, frontiersmen needed relatives and dependable friends who would come to their aid.

By 1879, the cattle drives were coming to an end. Kansas towns were therefore less willing to pay good salaries to peace officers. Wyatt began talking with his father and brothers about the future. They decided to return to Nicholas's ranch in Colton, California. Since the U.S. Army had at last defeated the Comanche and Apache tribes, who had fought to keep their lands, the Santa Fe Trail was again open. This southern route to California was much shorter than the Oregon Trail. More important, railroad tracks were being laid through the Gila River valley, which had been bought from Mexico in 1853 in the Gadsen Purchase. Because Colton would be

Loading ore at a mine in the Tombstone district in the early 1880s was no easy matter, as this photo taken by photographer Camilius S. Fly shows. Mules are lined up to drag away the heavy load.

*When the prospector John Schieffelin told soldiers that he would eventually find something out there in the desert, they laughed and said, "Yes, your tombstone." In 1877, when he founded the city in the desert after discovering a vast silver mine, he named it Tombstone. In on the joke, John Clum, a successful Indian agent turned newspaperman, called his Tombstone paper the* **Daily Epitaph.**

connected to the East by the Southern Pacific railroad line, Nicholas was eager to return to his ranch in Colton, California, which would soon be worth much more money. In May 1879, Nicholas Earp led his wagon train out of Dodge City and down the Santa Fe Trail. Nicholas, Morgan, and Warren Earp made the trip all the way to Colton, but Virgil and his wife, Allie, stopped in Prescott, the capital of Arizona Territory, where he found employment at a sawmill and as a constable. Soon Virgil wrote his brothers about Tombstone, Arizona, a rough mining town not far from the Mexican border where silver had recently been discovered.

Later that summer, at Virgil's suggestion, Wyatt and Mattie, with Jim and

his family, started for Tombstone with a string of horses. They probably rode the Santa Fe Railroad to the end
of the line in New Mexico, where they picked up Doc
Holliday and his fiery, independent-minded girlfriend,
Kate Elder. By wagon, they then proceeded to Prescott,
where Morgan joined them. When the Earps drove into
Tombstone, they saw a small town filled with opportunities. The Arizona Territory was wide open and the
prospects for making money were very real for anyone
with courage and ambition. Moreover, John Charles
Frémont, a Republican and a former Union general, was
governor of the territory. The Earps had good reason to
believe that he would look favorably on Republicans
who happened to be Union veterans and who had experience in law enforcement.

# 5. Tombstone

By late November 1879, the Earp brothers were reunited in Tombstone. In the meantime, Virgil had been named deputy U.S. marshal. He was even-tempered, dependable, and he had the look of a man who could take care of himself. The Earps probably lived in primitive conditions at first. Until wooden buildings were built, everyone in Tombstone lived in tents.

Virgil Earp wore a deputy U.S. marshal's badge, like this one.

In early 1880, as news of the opportunities in Tombstone spread, the town grew from a population of nine hundred to two thousand, yet the city was so compact that a short walk in any direction from the central business district quickly led to the livery stables and the corrals on the edge of town. The Earps settled down to make money. Jim opened a bar and gaming house. Happy-go-lucky Morgan rode shotgun on a stagecoach. The baby of the family, Warren, came later and was

Wells Fargo was the most prominent shipping and banking firm in the West. Wyatt Earp secretly worked for them in Tombstone, Arizona, helping to protect their stagecoaches from thieves. The building pictured here, on the remains of Main Street in the ghost town of Silver Roof, Utah, was completed around 1879.

employed by Virgil for routine tasks that involved little danger. This frustrated him to no end. He was so hot-tempered, in fact, that the family referred to him as the Tiger. Wyatt had intended to open a stage line to bring in supplies and to carry away silver, but a company named Wells Fargo was already established as the dominant shipping and banking firm. Not discouraged, Wyatt quickly made a secret arrangement with Wells Fargo to protect their interests against outlaws and thieves. He became deputy sheriff, a duty more important than it

Prospectors with no training in geology or chemistry might stake claims on good sites, but extracting silver from ore required expert knowledge. Moreover, only those with sufficient money to hire laborers, to buy machinery, and to wait for results could expect to make a profit. Consequently, the development of western mines, railroads, banking, and even ranching relied on eastern and European investors, that is, on capitalists. Investing in such enterprises was risky. Therefore, investors relied on large profits from those ventures that were successful to balance out those that lost money. Some investors got rich, many more got moderate returns, and some lost everything.

sounds because the sheriff was 75 miles (121 km) away, in Tucson, Arizona. Wyatt's duties included tax collecting, driving away squatters from city lots, and expelling claim jumpers who used force and threats to take over mine sites. Most of the time he did not carry a weapon. His was not yet a dangerous job, nor was he particularly interested in law enforcement. He wanted to make his fortune through investments in mines and other property. Being deputy sheriff provided him with a good salary in the meantime, and it allowed him to talk with people who understood the mining business.

Tombstone's real money was in silver, but finding it was difficult and mining it was hard work. Furthermore, there were Apaches and outlaws, both ready to kill unwary prospectors and miners. The Earps were speculators. They would buy shares in mines that had not yet been opened and sell to other investors when silver was found. Wyatt made quite a bit of money from these investments. At first this prosperity did little to affect day-to-day life in the family's small, dirt-floor shack. The Earp wives struggled to find firewood and to haul water from an outside well. They never forgot the labor and the humiliation of taking in other people's laundry in the summer heat and dust. In addition, they were socially isolated. None of the four Earp women, wives of saloon keepers, gamblers, and lawmen, were accepted by polite society. Consequently, not one of them had fond memories of the twenty-six months they lived in Tombstone. The men made do at first with slender incomes, but as they began to make money, they built small, individual houses and bought some expensive luxuries. Everything was expensive at first, because even necessities had to be hauled into town over mountainous terrain.

The town lay on a rolling, dry plain of thin grass, surrounded by distant wooded mountains and rough country. The wind never seemed to stop, and it was always hot. Streets were either dusty or muddy, and horse manure could be avoided only by staying on the wooden sidewalks. After the arrival of the railroad from Tucson in March, Tombstone grew rapidly. By the end of 1880, six thousand people had crowded into hastily constructed houses and hotels. Restaurants, drug-stores, bakeries, hotels, harness and shoe stores, ten cigar stores, one ice cream saloon, two banks, and a pho-tography gallery soon opened. There were two newspa-pers, the Democratic *Nugget* and the Republican *Daily Epitaph*, and sixty saloons. Within a year the population would swell to perhaps eight thousand.

Those who had not struck it rich mining silver found life hard and dollars scarce in the growing town of Tombstone. Even the outlaws found life difficult. Many

---

*Opposite*: Here is a replica of the *Daily Epitaph*, Tombstone's newspa-per, a few days after the famous gunfight at the O.K. Corral. It was printed on October 30, 1881. The advertisements on the right side of the page give an idea of what life was like in Tombstone.

## WEEKLY MINING REPORT

### An Exceedingly Quiet Week in Mining Circles.

**Huachuca Letter.**

We introduce our mining report to-day with an interesting letter from a much neglected mineral country; a country that is destined ere long to attract both energy and capital, which, from all reports, will be amply repaid for all outlays. The Huachuca mountains are the most prominent land-mark in Cochise county, and offer every facility for profitable mining, there being an abundance of wood and water and easy of access from every side. The Atchison, Topeka & Santa Fe Railroad passes up the Barbacomari valley, near the north end of the range, which will give transportation almost to their doors. This is a matter of great importance, from the fact that there are extensive copper mines that, when developed, will demand cheap rates for coke and copper. There are also carbonate deposits, both rich and extensive, which will make a like demand. Our correspondent says:

EDITOR EPITAPH—In accordance with your suggestions I will submit a few points about the western slope of the Huachuca Mountains at the further end of Tanner's Canyon. This part of the country has been slighted thus far by capitalists, owing possibly to its remoteness and inducements on the eastern slope. The Huachucas have been cried down as base, and by many condemned in a wholesale manner, simply because their interests are elsewhere, but the time is coming when their true merit will be recognized and the former unjust prejudices will change to just praise.

A first-class wagon road leads from Charleston to Tanner's Canyon on this side, the lowest depression in the range as viewed from Tombstone, into which picturesque and romantic canyon one drives several miles and then crosses by a good trail, horseback, to the west side, passing Hayes & Tanner's sawmill near the summit, where lumber is prepared for the Harshaw market. On the descending slope are some promising properties, and at the foot and in the heart of the deep canyon is a four-stamp quartz mill in fine running order, and which has lately tested some of the various ores with flattering results, using copper plates to catch the free gold, which is quite plentiful in the iron pyrites with which the sumberless ledges are well seamed. Wood and water are both abundant and plentiful, lessening the expense of milling materially, and high hopes are entertained of this now comparatively lonely locality soon budding into a very promising mining camp. And why not? The ledges are strong and well defined, running generally north and south with a pitch west, and although some blankets are found, the indications of true fissure veins are very apparent, and when work has been done by the prospectors to any extent, the claims promise well and offer great inducements to capital to take hold and continue the development. Limited development is going on, but not in a manner to show much results, one way or the other. Limited funds means limited work, and one can not expect to pay as he goes in this more than in any other business. Capital must be invested judiciously and the risk taken, and as a mining risk the Huachucas offer superior inducements.

In conclusion, I beg leave to differ from those holding the opinion that the ores can not be successfully milled, as experience teaches the contrary when the mines and ore is considered, that the tailings will not be lost to the former. After running a while and run through the pan and retort, the greatest percentage possible is had, as the sulphurets can not be worked in any other way more economically. I shall be glad to furnish information at any time to any one before returning to the mountains the middle of next week.

Very truly yours,
GEORGE WHITWELL PARSONS.

**Tombstone M. & M. Co.**

No. 2 shaft West Side, the vein has increased to 4½ feet, all ore of fine quality. The drift is in north on the ledge 30 feet. Are working only 9 men, including surface men, and taking out 26 tons of ore per week, which goes forward to the mill. This ore is all extracted in the legitimate way of development by running the drift upon the vein. Counting the ore at $50 per ton (a very low estimate for this ledge) the product is $1300 per week, less mining expenses, $252; which leaves a balance of net ore value at the mine of $1328. Body of ore in Tough Nut on 200 level getting superficially larger and thicker as the developments proceed. It is of the regular uniform Tough Nut ore, running about $60 to the ton. Work in the old mine east of the northwest shaft, shows the ore body going down to the level of the northwest workings. The Combination continues to yield its accustomed amount of ore. The developments for the last month have been more favorable than for any preceding period in the history of the mine, and there are more good ore bodies exposed at any former period. The mills are working at their full capacity and will make a good monthly showing.

**Contention.**

Are still drifting north on 212 level, all in good ore. On 312 north drift same ore body as above and equally rich. Sinking winze on this ore body from 312 to connect with 400. Full size of winze is 14½ feet. On still drifting on 400 and raising to connect with 312. Making from 35 to 40 feet in the various drifts per week. There is no change on 400 level, where cross-cutting still goes on. Are passing through a kindly ledge matter, which indicates that ore will be found at an early day. The stopes are all looking well, and show a plenty of rich ore everywhere. The mill is running smoothly, and up to its full capacity. The bullion output will be short, owing to the break in the engine in the early part of the month, which caused a stoppage of one whole week. However, with the surplus in the treasury, we anticipate no suspension of dividends for the month. We expect to record the payment of $900,000 in dividends the current year.

**Head Center.**

There have been no new developments for the past week. Prospecting on the first and second levels is being pushed ahead with good results. Taking out the usual amount of ore, which goes forward to the mill. The mill has been working steadily during the month. Have just completed a new cage, that is as fine a specimen of forging and workmanship as can be turned out anywhere. The safety cap is a half circle, made of three-sixteenths the boiler plate, opening in the center, one-half dropping down upon either side to admit of handling long timbers upon the cage. When closed, the joint is only just perceptible. It reflects great credit

upon the maker, as it is one of those jobs of piece work sandwiched in between tool sharpening.

**Grand Central.**

New shaft down 35 feet below 300 level. The rock is harder, slower progress being the result. Cross-cut on 300 level in 10 feet. Drifting south on 200. Old shaft down 24 below the 300 level. Will put in station on 380 this week, when cross-cutting will be commenced to prospect this level. An important point will be settled this week, and that is, whether the same level in the various mines on the Contention lode will develop water. Head Center struck a heavy flow near or at 500 feet; Grand Central is 87 feet higher; therefore the 600 level will be equivalent to a little more in the Head Center. If no water is struck about this point it will be conclusive evidence that the water veins in the fissure are controlled by the nature of the formation and vary in depth accordingly. This is fairly demonstrated already in Silver Belt, which struck water at about 187 feet. The difference in altitude between Head Center and Silver Belt is not over 25 or 30 feet.

In the stopes there is no material change. There is plenty of ore in sight and of a good quality. The mill is running satisfactorily and the out-put will be up to last month. The new ore house will be raised this week and finished as rapidly as possible.

**San Diego.**

During the month have added 10 feet to the depth of the shaft. Drifted south on the ledge 12 feet at the 265 ft. level, and have cross-cut 12 feet to the east at the same level. The cross-cut is still in porphyry which is heavily stained and contains iron pyrites in great abundance. No work has been done during the month at the 180 ft. level, although both drifts show a strong ledge of low grade quartz. The north drift has been run but 40 ft., improving in appearance and richness with every foot of advance.

**Prompter.**

Down 200 feet in shaft No. 3. Put in station on Monday last and are cross-cutting the vein. In 15 feet, cutting for the hanging wall. It is all medium grade ore, assaying from $40 to $60 per ton. It is all being saved for the mill. Drifting continues at the rate of about 2 feet a day. Grading for hoisting works, which will be erected as soon as it arrives from Chicago, where built.

**Horseshoe.**

Drift on 220 level in 45 feet. The rock which is porphyry and talc, works well and good headway is being made. The strike of the Emily and other veins is in a direction toward this location. The formation is all that could be desired, in fact, so identical with the entire central and eastern system of ledges and deposits that at any point almost there is a liability to meet an ore body.

**Ruby.**

Down 100 feet. Cross-cut at 50 feet; is 8 feet; all ledge matter, with 18 inches of high grade ore. Cross-cutting at 100 feet, drifting to the vein. Have to run between 15 and 20 feet. Started work on shaft No. 2, on Monday last and are down 18 feet. Sinking on the vein, the whole size of shaft in ledge matter with some fine ore.

**Mose Consolidated.**

Down 135 feet. The increase in size of boulders indicates the near approach to bedrock. There has been more quartz in the debris for the last week, and the fine earth has a more mineralized appearance. Assays will be made from it to test the question as to whether it carries silver or not.

**Silver Belt.**

Still crosscutting to the west. The rock is harder than some feet back. The drift is in 190 feet. The country is a mixture of lime, porphyry, black spar and talc. It is more kindly in appearance than for some feet back.

**Vizina.**

There is really nothing new to report from this mine. Everything runs along so smoothly from week to week that what was written one week ago would answer for this week. The usual progress was made and the ore bodies all yield as heretofore.

**Huachuca Water Company.**

From Mr. L. J. Gird, engineer of the works, it is learned that the rip-rap for the reservoir has been completed, and the whole work will soon be finished. It will not take long to lay the pipe when it arrives. The catchment reservoir was the heaviest work on the line.

**BISBEE.**

**Atlanta.**

Work was started up on this mine last week. A tunnel was started on the west side to be used for the croppings near the Copper Queen. The prospects are considered first-class.

**Golden Gate.**

A shaft was started in the iron cap that crosses this location on the 4th instant, and has been sunk to a depth of 14 feet. As it feet a vein of carbonate ore 3 inches thick came in, and at the bottom it had widened to over two feet. This promises to be a rich mine.

**TUCSON SMALL TALK.**

*Star.*

The Board of Supervisors will meet on Tuesday, November 1st.

The District Court will open in Tombstone November 14th.

Carlilo Meyer, the young son of Judge Meyer, is ill with typhoid fever.

Dr. H. Ming has been appointed Public Administrator of Graham county.

Solon M. Allis is on his way back from the East.

The Fleishman-Meyer wedding comes off next Monday night.

The Cochise Board of Supervisors seem disposed to take their own time in bringing their settlement with Pima county to a focus.

Hebert Bible, who is charged with killing Bulos, his step-father in Pinal county, is transferred to Tucson, on a change of venue, and is now in jail here. He was formerly a pupil in a school taught by Mr. George A. Chase, and now the friends of George are inquiring how far he becomes accessory before the fact in Bible's offense, he being in some measure responsible for Bible's moral training. It is all proper enough "to teach the young idea how to shoot," but not in this particular aboriginal way.

A COSTA de Baca, corner of Fifth and Allen streets, have the largest and most complete stock of Tobacco and Cigars to be found in Tombstone. They keep the finest as well as common brands, and sell wholesale and retail.

**CORONER'S INQUEST.**

**Conclusion of the Evidence, with the Verdict of the Jury.**

At 10 o'clock yesterday morning the examination of witnesses before the Coroner's Jury was continued.

First witness called was

F. D. FELLEY,

who testified as follows: After the shooting commenced, saw Holliday in the middle of the street, and the youngest of the Earps about three feet from the sidewalk; he was firing at a man behind a horse; Holliday was also firing at the same man; Holliday was also firing at a man who had run by him to the opposite side of the street. Then I saw the man who held the horse let go the bridle and keep staggering until he fell, his back within a few feet of a house; had a pistol in his hand, but I did not see it go off; did not see the other two Earps at this time; went and offered to pick up the wounded man; he did not speak, though his lips moved; picked up a revolver laying about three feet from him and placed it by his side; this was on the north side of Fremont street. Saw one Holliday running towards where the man was lying; had his pistol in his hand; he said, "The son of a b—bit me—I mean to kill him." Holliday did not shoot after saying this; did not see a shot over three; Earp and Holliday aid; the Earps coming down the street; Holliday had a gun; I heard the man on the outside say to Holliday, "Let them have it," and Holliday said, "All right." That is all I know.

P. H. COLEMAN

testified. I saw the arrest of Ike Clanton before the shooting. Marshal Earp went up behind and grabbed his gun, then there was a scuffle, and Clanton fell. Did not see Earp hit him. Saw Earp have a six-shooter, but don't know if he took it from Clanton or not. He then took Clanton to the police court. After the trial was over, Earp offered Clanton his rifle, but Clanton did not take it. Heard Clanton say all he wanted was four feet of ground. Soon after I was walking down on the north side of Fremont street I saw two men coming from the direction of the O.K. Corral. Billy Clanton was on horseback and Frank McLowry was leading his horse. As they passed me, Billy Clanton said, "Where's the West End Corral?" Told him where it was. They passed through the corral and I walked up Allen street. Met Sheriff upon the Headquarters Saloon and said in joke, "You should disarm those men; they are up to some mischief." Soon after Marshal Earp and told him the same thing. After this met the Clantons and McLowry opposite Fly's on Fremont street. Sheriff Behan was talking to them. One of them said, "You need not be afraid of us, Johnny; we will make no trouble." Billy Clanton had his horse with him. I turned and walked up Fremont street. I met two Earps and Doc Holliday opposite Bauer's meat market. Just as they passed me, Behan stepped out of Wyatt Earp's house. As I walked away he said, "Billy Clanton has his horse with him, and he says he came to town on business, and he will go out of town directly." After the first two shots, Ben McLowry was standing by his horse on the sidewalk, with his hand on his gun; he then reeled over; you have described; I am here to answer for what I have done. Saw Billy Clanton with his hand on his pistol, which was in the scabbard; his right hand was on the left hip. This was after the first two shots; could not swear how many of the Clantons were armed; don't think Ike was; the boys say not; jumping up again, he commenced firing. At this time saw Frank McLowry advancing toward Holliday and saying "I've got you now," firing a shot at the same time. That shot struck Holliday on the hip. Frank passed on across the street and fell. Billy Clanton, after being struck, had been down on the ground, got up and fell, and I heard him say, "Give it to them, give it to them." Don't think there was anybody but the Marshal who arrested the Clantons. Believe the report I gave the Sheriff was about correct. Can't say that I saw a shotgun in the hands of either party. Thank Holliday had a shotgun, believe the parties were about 5 or 10 feet apart when shooting commenced; saw Holliday with a nickel-plated pistol; the mornings I went and saw Wyatt Earp; I asked him if he had been hit; he said no; I saw no shotgun at that time, but his man with the hand on his gun. Doc Holliday came running and saw Mac gun Earp; had his gun in his hand; don't know whether the ball came from the crowd or some other gun. I looked around but saw no other body; there was nothing between the Earps and the boys that morning. There were men on the side walks down there; they don't like me. There were no threats made against the Earps by any one that morning. I heard that they were all afraid of one another. Wyatt Earp and myself were the two nearest the boys when the shooting commenced. The first two shots were fired so near together you could not tell which were fired first. Billy Clanton and Frank McLowry were the first ones killed. After the shooting was over, I went up and saw some one take hold of Morg. Earp; did not see Virg. Earp; Wyatt Earp and Morgan Earp were the first I saw shot; did not see him shoot but once; Wyatt and Morg. Earp stepped out to meet them, and said "I want your pistols;" I told him that I had no gun. Looking around I saw Morgan Earp fall to the ground and get up again; I saw the Marshal also said to them "Throw up your hands." I only heard the one expression. Came back soon and played poker with Virg. Earp, Doc McLowry and others. Virg. told me when he returned from arrest he told me of a b—n; the last I saw of him was the last I saw before he was killed. Came back soon and played poker with Virg. Earp, Doc McLowry and others. He said he thought he was shot. I put the first two shots so near together you could not tell which was fired first. Cannot state positively who fired the first shot.

**The following is the verdict of the Coroner's Jury:**

We, the undersigned, a jury of inquest, summoned by the Coroner of the county aforesaid, to determine when the bodies are, submitted to the inspection, and under what circumstances they came to death; after viewing the bodies and hearing such testimony as has been submitted to us, find, first, that the persons' names were, William Clanton, aged 18 years, Frank McLowry, aged 35 years, and Tom McLowry, aged 35 years, natives unknown, and that they came to their death in the town of Tombstone, in said county, on the 26th day of October, 1881, from the effects of pistol and gunshot wounds inflicted by Virgil Earp, Morgan Earp and one Holliday, commonly called Doc Holliday.    [Signed] Thomas Moses, T. F. Hudson, D. Calisher, N. Garrett, S. B. Comstock, J. W. Conwell, J. C. Oauls, C. D. Rep.py, F. Hofford, George H. Haskell, M. V. Moodrich.

Johnny Ringo, born John Peters Ringgold on May 3, 1850, was part of the cowboy ring in Tombstone. Many believe Ringo tried to avenge the cowboys who died at the O.K. Corral gunfight. He died under mysterious circumstances in 1882 and was buried beside West Turkey Creek, where his body was found. The location is on private property on Sander's Ranch in southeastern Arizona.

of the so-called cowboys, who had herded cattle from Texas to Kansas, had been chased out of Texas by the Rangers or out of New Mexico by the range wars, which were violent conflicts between ranchers and organized gangs of cattle thieves. A few cowboys had taken jobs as hands, or hired help, on Arizona ranches. Many more rustled stock, that is, stole cattle, from large American and Mexican ranches, slipping across the border to avoid being caught. The cowboys even had a leader, Curly Bill Brocius. The gunslinger of the group was Johnny Ringo, a brooding loner with a reputation as a killer. The cowboys sold their stolen cattle and horses to ambitious ranchers like the Clanton and McLaury families, who then sold them to the citizens of Tombstone. The cowboys' claim that they stole only from the rich, not from small ranchers, caused some people to think of them as Robin Hood figures, but their popularity might have rested more on their Confederate pasts. Their southern backgrounds, however, did not endear them to Texas-born ranchers like John Slaughter, who had been the first to open a cattle trail through West Texas to Colorado and who did not like being robbed. Such rivalries between cowboys and ranchers were not uncommon, but in Tombstone they lacked the mutual tolerance based on business arrangements. In addition, the conflict now involved federal officers who were ordered to protect Mexican citizens from rustlers and outlaws. After the massacre at the Alamo in 1835, there were few cowboys

The Alamo, shown here, was an old Spanish mission outside of San Antonio. It was converted to a fort during the many battles for Mexican and Texas independence. The fort was defended by only a handful of men in 1835, who fought valiantly, but in the end they were all killed.

*"Remember the Alamo" was the motto adopted by Texans in 1835 after the Mexican dictator Antonio López de Santa Anna had executed the survivors of a battle outside San Antonio. Although the Texans won the war, Mexico refused to recognize Texas as an independent republic. Relations between Texans and Mexicans remained tense for many years thereafter. Santa Anna later returned to power and in 1853, sold what became southern Arizona, the Gadsen Purchase, to the United States so that he could pay his debts to political friends.*

who saw Mexicans in any way other than as enemies of Texas, and they enjoyed stealing cattle from them.

Cattle rustling might have remained a rural problem if Tombstone had not needed cheap beef for the miners. Political life was dominated by the County Ring, a political gang headed by John Harris Behan, an Irish Democrat whose policy was to talk big and to do little. Behan had been in Arizona Territory since 1863, and he either knew everybody or made it a point to introduce himself. Cynics referred to Behan and his friends as the Ten Percent Ring, a reference to the cut they took as tax collectors. Behan also had a spirited girlfriend, Josephine Sarah Marcus, a singer and a dancer from San Francisco. She went by the nickname Sadie. Their relationship was stormy, because Josephine was jealous of the attention Behan gave to other women. When she returned to Tombstone in October 1880 from a visit home, she was ready to leave him. At the same time, Wyatt's relationship with Mattie was breaking up. Wyatt and Josephine would eventually fall in love, and many believe that Behan never forgave Wyatt for stealing her away.

In July 1880, when Arizona's blistering heat was at its hottest, someone stole six mules from Camp Rucker, a nearby U.S. Army base. A lieutenant from the camp asked the local deputy U.S. marshal, Virgil Earp, to look for the thief. Virgil quickly deputized Wyatt and Morgan, and the three men set off for the McLaury ranch. There they discovered a branding iron that would change brands from

Courtesy of Stephen and Marge Elliott, Tombstone Western Heritage Museum

Josephine Sarah Marcus, or Josie Earp, is pictured here in 1879 when she was 18 years old. Originally engaged to John Behan, Josephine ended up with Wyatt Earp. This might have been the beginning of the bitter rivalry between Earp and Behan. This rare photograph is by Camilius S. Fly, of Tombstone, Arizona, who was a photographer and a lawman. Fly documented many people and scenes of frontier life, especially of rapidly growing Tombstone.

US to D8. This was good evidence that the army mules were at the ranch. The lieutenant, however, tried to avoid a conflict by accepting the McLaurys' word that they would return the mules. Afterward the McLaurys publicly insulted the Earps in person and in letters to the *Nugget*, and, of course, they never gave the lieutenant the mules.

This was a critical moment for the Earps. They had stumbled upon a large-scale criminal organization that was ruining many ranchers, but which had ties to local politicians and merchants. Therefore they could not be prosecuted easily. The Earps were Republicans and veterans of the Union army. The cowboys were Democrats and former Confederates. What should the Earps do?

This is a nineteenth century U.S. Army branding iron. An iron like this would have been used in Arizona during Earp's time.

To go up against the cowboys would be dangerous, and it was clearly in the Earps' own business interests to let the matter drop. The Earps' decision to enforce the law ultimately led to the most famous gunfight in history.

# 6. The Gunfight at the O.K. Corral

In the fall of 1880, Wyatt was a solid citizen of Tombstone. He was deputy sheriff, and the job provided a good income. He was also the operator of the gambling concessions in several saloons, an investor in several mining companies, and an undercover agent for Wells Fargo. Some citizens came to believe that Wyatt and his brothers were less than honest, and that they also made money as con artists. However, the line between legal and illegal activities was less clear on the frontier than it was back in the East.

Doc Holliday had stayed in Prescott, Arizona, to gamble until he saw that Wyatt needed help. Soon after arriving in Tombstone, Doc made enemies of the cowboys. Doc was an extremely skilled card player, and the cowboys lost a lot of money to him. Poker was not a game for amateurs, like the cowboys, who did not play every day as

Doc Holliday probably played cards with some like this one made at the end of the nineteenth century in London.

did professional gamblers. However, the cowboys thought they were losing because Doc was cheating. Wyatt protected his friend against these accusations, and Wyatt's relationship with the cowboys grew worse.

The bad feelings between the cowboys and the Earps boiled over in October 1880, when Curly Bill Brocius fatally shot Marshal Fred White. Wyatt instantly clubbed Brocius over the head and arrested him for murder, but Brocius argued successfully to a Tucson judge that the gun had gone off by accident. Virgil Earp took on Marshal White's duties, but lost the election that November to Behan's candidate.

Wyatt's prized racing horse had been stolen shortly after the Earps had arrived in Tombstone. Acting on a tip, Wyatt and Doc Holliday rode to the Clanton ranch in nearby Charleston, where they found the animal. Billy Clanton was a teenager with an attitude, and although he let Wyatt ride away with the horse, he told Wyatt and everyone within hearing distance what he thought of him. In November, Wyatt resigned his position as deputy sheriff without giving any reason for his decision. Johnny Behan replaced him, and when a new district, Cochise County, was created for the Tombstone area, Behan persuaded Governor Frémont to appoint him sheriff. Behan may have promised Wyatt an undersheriff's appointment if Wyatt did not seek to become sheriff himself, and Wyatt probably understood that the Democratic legislature would never have approved a

Republican for the office anyway. If Behan made such a promise, he quickly went back on his word.

The previous sheriff, who resided in distant Tucson, had relied on Wyatt to enforce the law, and Doc Holliday had backed Wyatt. Now, however, Behan was living in Tombstone, and he was in league with the cowboys and the McLaury and Clanton ranchers. It was not in his best interest to enforce the law. However, Virgil remained a deputy U.S. marshal. Wyatt became Virgil's deputy and therefore was still a threat to the cowboys' illegal operations.

In January 1881, Wyatt arrested cowboy leader Johnny Ringo for murder, protected him from a lynch mob, and then had to stand by as charges were dropped. This frustrated Wyatt. No matter how many cowboys he arrested, he couldn't keep any of them behind bars where they belonged. Several months after the arrest of Ringo, the cowboys and the Earps were ready to kill one another. The feud grew worse when two men were slain during an attempted robbery of the Tombstone stage on March 15.

Virgil, Wyatt, Morgan, Bat Masterson, and a few others captured the man who had supplied horses for the robbers. They beat the names of the outlaws out of him, but they were unable to catch up with the gang before they crossed into New Mexico. In July, Sheriff Behan accused Doc Holliday of killing the shotgun guard of the stage and of participating in the robbery.

His charge was largely based on a drunken accusation by Kate, who had just had another fight with Doc. The charge was dropped when Wyatt produced witnesses who said that Doc was with them at the time of the robbery. Wyatt persuaded Kate to withdraw her statement. Despite Doc's proven innocence, rumors about the robbery spread. Enemies of the Earps began saying that Wyatt and his brothers were involved in the robbery, too. Hoping to get them put in jail or to drive them out of Tombstone, the cowboys went around saying that the Earps were crooks.

Wyatt, however, did not stop trying to enforce the law and to catch the real robbers. He made a deal with cowboy Ike Clanton to trick the robbers into coming back into Arizona. Wyatt would get credit for the arrest, and Ike would get the $6,000 reward. Ike, however, fearful that his outlaw friends would learn of his betrayal, backed out of the agreement. He then became terrified that Wyatt would tell people about their bargain.

Virgil was named city marshal in late June, and he immediately banned the carrying of weapons in town. His energetic search for stolen cattle and his feud with Behan, who kept trying to protect the cowboys from the law, made it obvious to everyone that trouble was coming. One of the major problems in law enforcement, then as now, is that of jurisdiction. As city marshal, Virgil Earp was responsible for dealing with criminal matters inside Tombstone. Sheriff Behan was responsible

© Collection of the New-York Historical Society/40746

Joseph Isaac "Ike" Clanton, pictured here in the only photo known to exist of him, tried to open a restaurant when he first came to Tombstone, Arizona. It was not successful. He was born in Missouri, in 1847, but his family came to the West looking for new opportunities.

for rural crimes. Putting a stop to rustling should have been the sheriff's responsibility, but since Behan was not willing to act against the cowboys, the task fell to Virgil Earp, who could also act as deputy U.S. marshal. In July 1881, Virgil heard that cattle stolen from Mexico were at the Clanton ranch. He immediately formed a posse and investigated. No charges were filed, but the cowboys were outraged again.

In August, Mexican troops crossed the border in search of cowboys who had ambushed a party of Mexican silver smugglers. When they found a camp of sleeping cowboys, they attacked. Among the dead in the Guadalupe Canyon Massacre was the aged Newton Clanton, whom everybody called Old Man Clanton. Rumor had it that the Earps had worked with the Mexicans, and that both Doc Holliday and Warren Earp had been wounded in the battle. Although that was unlikely, Doc did disappear for a few weeks and Warren left for Colton. Afterward Ike Clanton accused Doc Holliday of killing his father.

In September, there was another stagecoach robbery. Wyatt arrested Frank Stilwell, Behan's chief deputy, for the crime. When Stillwell went free, there was talk in town about the failure of the judicial system. It looked as if vigilante justice would happen at any minute. Vigilantes were dangerous, especially miners, who were accustomed to protecting their group interests violently. Many people were furious

Tom McLaury was part of a ranching
family in Tombstone that sold cattle
stolen by the cowboys for a nice profit.

that the cowboys were getting away with their criminal activities and thought they should be hunted down and killed. The Earps wanted to prosecute the cowboys, but they also did not want the mob to take over.

On October 25, Ike Clanton and Tom McLaury rode into Tombstone on their wagon and began drinking heavily. By this time, the Clantons, the McLaurys, and the cowboys were fed up with the Earps getting in the way of their business. Ike was soon talking wildly, saying that he wanted a shoot-out with Holliday and the Earps. After an all-night poker game with Tom McLaury, Virgil Earp, and Sheriff Behan, Ike gave Virgil a message for Holliday that he had better come out and fight. At noon Ike Clanton was on the main street, drunk, waving a rifle, and yelling threats. Virgil came up behind him and knocked him out with his revolver. The justice of the peace, however, was satisfied with assessing Clanton a twenty-five-dollar fine. Meanwhile, Tom McLaury, searching for Clanton, saw

*The O.K. Corral was a reference to Old Kinderhook, the hometown of Martin Van Buren, who was elected president on the Democratic ticket in 1840. The O.K. Corral slowly lost its political message. Contemporaries, however, understood the name as a promise of fine services to the common people, who were mostly Democrats, the majority party in Arizona Territory.*

Wyatt and insulted him. Wyatt struck him over the head and disarmed him. Frustrated by the corrupt and ineffective judicial system, Wyatt left McLaury bleeding in the street instead of taking him to the judge. Soon the Clantons and the McLaurys were seen at the gunshop, rearming themselves. The Earps and the cowboys stared at one another across the street until Virgil led his brothers down to the Wells Fargo office to get his shotgun.

By 2:00 P.M. on October 26, 1881, the streets were lined with onlookers. When Virgil ordered the cowboys to leave town, they went to the O.K. Corral to get their horses, but not before making more threats against the Earps.

Armed citizens who had heard Ike Clanton's repeated threats had meanwhile begun to gather, saying that if the law would not act against the cowboys, they would. When Virgil heard that the cowboys had left the O.K. Corral but remained in town, armed and shouting threats, he decided to end the matter before a mob could get involved.

At 2:30 P.M., the Earps began their fateful walk from Allen Street down Fourth Street. When Sheriff Behan came out to stop them, Virgil invited him to assist in

Courtesy of Stephen and Marge Elliott, Tombstone Western Heritage Museum

This vacant lot, between Fly's Rooming House (on the right) and the Harwood cottage (behind the mule), is where the historic O.K. Corral gunfight occurred on October 26, 1881. This rarely seen image is believed to have been taken prior to a fire in May 1882, which burned a number of Tombstone properties, including Fly's Rooming House. This scene shows the O.K. Corral gunfight area as it actually looked at the time of the shooting, making the print a remarkable find.

disarming the cowboys. Behan declined. Shortly there-after, Doc Holliday stopped the Earps in the street. He exchanged a few harsh words with Wyatt, who had wanted to keep him out of the business. He then per-suaded the Earps to take him along. Wyatt wasn't sure how many cowboys they would have to face, and having a skilled gunfighter like Holliday could only help their chances.

Virgil handed his shotgun to Holliday, who hid the weapon under his overcoat. Virgil then took Holliday's cane so that he would look less threatening when he asked the cowboys for their weapons. Walking steadily around the corner onto Fremont Street, Virgil, Wyatt, Morgan, and Doc Holliday saw Johnny Behan and the five cowboys, Ike and Billy Clanton, Tom and Frank McLaury, and Billy Claiborne. The cowboys retreated into a vacant lot, while Behan ran up to the Earps, shouting that he couldn't allow violence. When the Earps walked right past him, he took cover.

When the Earps turned into the vacant lot, the cow-boys were not ready for a fight. Tom McLaury may have been getting on his horse to leave, or he might have been going after the rifle that was attached to his saddle.

---

*Next Page*: Wyatt Earp drew this diagram of the shoot-out at the O.K. Corral in the 1900s with John Flood Jr., for Stuart Lake's book on Wyatt Earp. In it he gives the position of all the men involved in the fight, according to the Earps' version of events.

Court House
@ Judge Butcherly[?]

Building

Fremont Street

19 oc Holliday

Jhn McLowry
Frank McLowry
Billy Clanton
Ike Clanton
Billy Claiborne

Wyatt Earp
M Earp
Virgil Earp

Third Street

Fourth Street

O K Corral

Allen Street

Diagram and lettering by J. H. B. Jr. — Dots designating
combatants by W. S. E. in street fight at Tombstone, Arizona,
October 26, 1881.
Wednesday September 15, 1926, 1:30 – 5:30 PM at 4000½ Mar. 196[?]
Los Angeles. — W. S. E. — J. H. B., Jr.
Over!                     Douglass St

When Virgil yelled, "Boys, throw up your hands!" Billy Claiborne and Ike Clanton took off. There was a confusion of voices. One cowboy might have cocked his single-action Colt revolver. Hearing the noise, Wyatt pulled his gun out of his overcoat pocket and fired. A simultaneous shot came from the moving ranks of the cowboys. Then the air was filled with lead, gunsmoke, and dust. Ike Clanton ran up to Wyatt, hands waving in the air, and tried to grab Wyatt's arm. Wyatt pushed him off and told him to "go to fighting or get away," then returned to the fight. Ike fled the scene, leaving his brother and friends to die. Thirty seconds after the first shot was fired, Billy Clanton and the two McLaury brothers lay dying. Virgil had been shot in the calf, Morgan across both shoulder blades, and Holliday along the hip. Only Wyatt remained untouched.

Johnny Behan then attempted to arrest the Earps, but Wyatt refused to allow it to happen. The next day's *Daily Epitaph* bore the headline: "Three Men Hurled into Eternity in the Duration of a Moment." The story was then picked up across the nation. Readers were stunned by the ferocity of the short battle. The legend of the Gunfight at the O.K. Corral had begun.

The coroner's inquest began two days later. Virgil was suspended as city marshal when Ike Clanton sought an indictment for murder. Historians still pore over the lengthy testimony in the trial that followed, but they are not in agreement as to what happened in

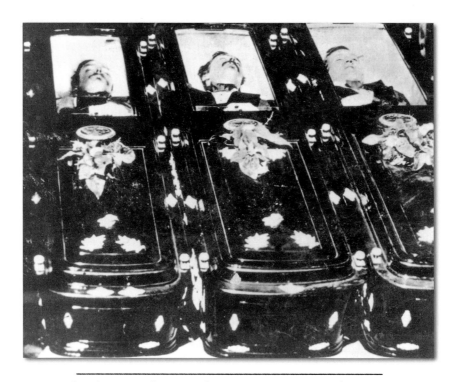

In this famous photograph, Tom McLaury, Frank McLaury, and Billy Clanton are shown in the aftermath of the O.K. Corral gunfight. According to a newspaper article in the *Nugget*, their funeral was the most impressive and the saddest sight ever witnessed in Tombstone.

that half-minute of gunfire and the events leading up to it. After a month of hearings, Justice of the Peace Will Spicer ruled that the Earps' conduct was justified and prudent.

If the Earps had left town at this moment, history would probably have been different. Josephine left, going back to her family in San Francisco. The gunfight made headlines around the nation. The story even made it into the papers in Wyatt's hometown, though it was significantly overshadowed by Buffalo

Bill's performance at a local opera house. By staying in town to protect their business interests, the Earps guaranteed that the feud with the cowboys would be fought to the end. They did not, however, expect the fight to go the way it did.

**Justice's Court.**

BEFORE JUSTICE SPICER.

In the case of Wyatt Earp, Morgan Earp, V. W. Earp and J. H. Holliday, charged with the murder of William Clanton, Thomas and Frank McLowry, on complaint filed by Isaac Clanton, the defendants Wyatt Earp and J. H. Holliday were refused bail as a matter of right. Said defendants were admitted to bail on showing by affidavit in the sum of $10,000 each, to appear for examination at 10 o'clock, Monday morning. Defendants gave bail, with sureties justifying in $20,000 in each case.

Pickled Pigs Feet' and Lambs' Tongues, at H. E. Hills & Co's.

This article printed in the *Daily Epitaph* a few days after the gunfight at the O.K. Corral gives information about the hearing the Earps and Holliday had in front of Justice Spicer. The trial would begin in earnest on the following Monday and would continue for many months.

# 7. The Vendetta Ride

On the night of December 28, 1881, three men ambushed Virgil in front of the Oriental Saloon. He lived, but his arm was permanently crippled from the shotgun blasts. The next day Wyatt persuaded the U.S. marshal to make him a deputy marshal. Clearly, there had to be some kind of law in Arizona Territory, and Sheriff Behan was not likely to provide it. Wyatt raised a posse and arrested Ike Clanton, who had lost his hat during the ambush, proving he was there. Ignoring the evidence, the judge dismissed the charges.

On the night of March 18, 1882, Morgan Earp was playing pool in Hatch's Saloon and Billiard Parlor when an assassin fired through the glass of the back door and killed him. Wyatt, who had been sitting nearby, felt a second bullet whiz past his head. The shooters escaped, but the coroner's jury did not hesitate to name four cowboys as the murderers. Wyatt made plans to evacuate Virgil and Allie from Tombstone for their safety.

Wyatt, Warren, Doc Holliday, and three deputies loaded Virgil and Allie, along with Morgan's body, onto

Wyatt Earp held an interest in the Oriental Saloon, pictured here, and often spent time there. It was in this saloon that the events of October 26 began and set in motion Wyatt's Vendetta Ride.

the train and accompanied them on the first leg of the journey to Colton. Expecting trouble, the party was heavily armed. As the train rolled into the station in Tucson, Wyatt saw several men on the platform armed with shotguns. Among them was Frank Stilwell, one of the suspected murderers. Stilwell's body was found near the train tracks the next morning. The circumstances were incriminating, leading most people to believe that the Earps were beginning to strike back. When Ike Clanton was able to obtain warrants against Wyatt and Warren Earp, Sheriff Behan promised to arrest them. The story became front-page news nation-wide, and it grew bigger in the days to follow as the Earps continued their Vendetta Ride.

Those who did not understand that the legal system had broken down condemned the Earps for taking the law into their own hands and for exercising vigilante justice. By the standards of the frontier, however, they were doing what Americans had done for generations whenever effective government was unable to provide protection to common citizens; they were standing up for themselves. All of their values urged them to defend themselves: loyalty to family, their sworn oaths to uphold the law, their sense of justice and fair play, and the frontier code of honor. It would be cowardly to back down or to run away. Whatever faults Wyatt Earp and his brothers had, lack of courage was not among them.

When the Earp party returned to Tombstone, Sheriff Behan made a weak effort to arrest them. The Earps, however, refused to surrender and rode out of town, easily losing Behan, who had raised a posse of twelve cowboys and set out in pursuit. Soon thereafter, the Earps killed one of Morgan's assassins, a man named Indian Charlie, and two days later Wyatt killed Curly Bill Brocius in a ferocious shoot-out. As the news spread across Arizona Territory, lawmen and vigilantes began to form new posses. Many Arizonans, confused by sensational newspaper stories, considered the Earps nothing more than another gang, one that was clearly out of control.

Mattie, who was still hanging around Tombstone, went to Colton at this time, possibly to stay out of the way. She never saw Wyatt again. She later settled in Pinal, Arizona, where she died in poverty.

Wyatt, Warren, and Doc Holliday left for Colorado, which was outside Arizona jurisdiction. When the governor of Colorado considered returning them to Arizona to stand trial, Bat Masterson persuaded him to leave them alone. Bat then began a very successful public relations campaign to present the Earps' side of the case in newspapers and magazines all across the country. Wyatt and Doc may have slipped back into Arizona in July 1882. At

This photo shows cell blocks at the historic, territorial prison in Yuma where John Behan would become superintendent.

This is a laudanum bottle from the late 1800s. The label calls it "Crest Brand Laudanum Poison."

After Mattie returned to Arizona, she became addicted to laudanum. This was a product made with opium, a common ingredient in over-the-counter painkillers. Many women became "hooked" on laudanum so thoroughly that eventually they could not tell where their disease left off and their addiction began. This was one of the reasons for the later passage of Pure Food and Drug laws. Mattie committed suicide in 1888.

least that is what people believed when Johnny Ringo was discovered with a bullet in his head. Wyatt joined Josephine in San Francisco in 1883, after which they went to Idaho with Jim. Doc Holliday remained in the Colorado Mountains, hoping that the dry air would cure his tuberculosis. He died a few years later. His last words were, "That's funny," perhaps referring to the fact that, after all of his many gun battles, he was going to die in bed.

The Earps lost all of their property in Tombstone, but Behan's career there was finished, too. Though his reputation was ruined, Behan later became superintendent of the Yuma Territorial Penitentiary. The Earps had hunted down and killed almost all the cowboys who were involved in Morgan's death and Virgil's shooting. When Ike Clanton was murdered in 1887, there was speculation, probably unfounded, that the Earps had finished the job.

# 8. Wyatt's Golden Years

Wyatt and Josephine were never separated again. Josephine became heavy, quarrelsome, and jealous as she aged. The other Earp women never accepted her, and she never had the children she had promised Wyatt. Nevertheless, Wyatt was happy. Their life together was relatively quiet, but hardly dull. They never lacked for money, though they rarely had much. Still their income was sufficient to support their footloose existence of prospecting, gambling, and racing horses in various mining towns across the West. For a while they lived in San Francisco. There Wyatt was a referee for boxing matches. He had learned the sport back in 1868 while working on a railroad construction gang. Consequently, he already had a reputation in boxing circles.

Wyatt's love of boxing got him involved in one of the most famous matches of the era, the Sharkey-Fitzsimmons fight in December 1896. There was much money riding on the match, and there was much suspicion that the referees were "fixed," that is, that they

Courtesy of Stephen and Marge Elliott, Tombstone Western Heritage Museum

The *San Francisco Call* printed an article on December 4, 1896, about the Sharkey-Fitzsimmons fight. Some of the headlines read, "The Courts Will Decide the Ownership of the Purse. Wyatt Earp Arrested Yesterday. A Majority of Sporting Men Still Believe That Fitzsimmons Was Robbed of the Decision and the Purse—Lynch's Statement."

had agreed to favor one fighter over the other. As a result, it was only at the last minute that the two boxers agreed on Wyatt Earp to judge the contest. When Fitzsimmons, the heavy favorite, succeeded in knocking Sharkey down, Wyatt ruled that this was a low blow and awarded the match to Sharkey. The Fitzsimmons crowd, having lost a fortune in bets, went wild. None of them had seen the punch! Fitzsimmons sued, but the judge threw out the suit on the grounds that prizefighting was illegal anyway.

*Wyatt's mother, Virginia Ann Cooksey Earp (1821–1893) was buried in the Colton, California, Pioneer Memorial cemetery. Her obituary in the* San Bernardino Daily Courier *on January 15, 1893, read: "Mrs. Earp was a loving and dutiful wife, a kind and indulgent mother, a quiet and peaceable citizen wherever she lived; was a lady of unimpeachable character; universally loved by all who knew her. To know her was to love her."*

Ever since then, an invisible low blow has been called a Wyatt Earp.

All in all, it was an embarrassing episode that reminded people of the O.K. Corral and the Vendetta Ride, events that Wyatt could not seem to escape. Newspaper stories and people across the West retold the story over and over again. Some painted Wyatt as the hero, others as a trigger-happy killer. The truth, however, was that Wyatt, although he often carried a weapon, was not in the habit of shooting men. He was never involved in a gunfight after he left Arizona, not even in Alaska, another wild frontier, where he lived from 1897 to 1900. Nevertheless, rumors went around that he had avenged Warren's death in 1900. Involved in several fights over the years, Warren was finally slain in a personal argument in Willcox, Arizona. The killer had successfully pled self-defense, but witnesses said that Warren had only attempted to disarm him. With Wyatt in Alaska, Virgil had probably taken revenge on behalf of the family.

Wyatt's father finally got his government pension for service in the Mexican War, though his claim that he had served in the Black Hawk War was rejected. Similarly, Nicholas's claim that he had recruited troops in the Civil War was never acknowledged. He died in an old soldiers' home in 1907. Wyatt's mother had died in Colton in 1893.

Wyatt and Josephine traveled from town to town across the West, often in the company of Wyatt's

Wyatt Earp was buried in the Hills of Eternity Memorial Park in Colma,
California. Josephine would be buried beside him when she died in
1944. A marker for Earp and Josephine in the same cemetery reads,
". . .There is nothing so sacred as honor, and nothing so loyal as love!"

brother Jim and sister Adelia. They later rented a
house in Los Angeles, where Wyatt Earp died on
January 13, 1929. Tom Mix and William S. Hart,
Hollywood's leading heroes of western "B" pictures,
were among the pallbearers.

Wyatt's acquaintance with great actors is one of the
most fascinating mysteries of his life. By the time
Hollywood had become a center for movie production,
Wyatt was too old to be an extra and he was too shy to
be an actor. Nevertheless, he somehow became

*A "B" western is generally thought of as
a low-budget movie made about the
American West. "B" westerns were agreed
to be well below the quality of "A"
pictures, but they were nevertheless
very popular. The formula was based less
on authentic western experience than on
the adventure novels of a German writer, Karl May,
whose only visit to America came long after
he wrote his books. May's superheroes
always had a wonder horse, unusual
weapons, a comic sidekick, and they always
regarded women as delicate creatures to
be protected but otherwise avoided.
May's stories became so influential
because several Hollywood producers
were emigrants from Germany who
had read Karl May's books in their youth.*

Courtesy of Stephen and Marge Elliott, Tombstone Western Heritage Museum

Wyatt Earp spent his later years in California and became friends with some of the actors who portrayed him in westerns. This photograph was taken August 9, 1923. Wyatt was 75 years old.

acquainted with some of the most important western stars of the era. He visited some movie sets, but he always remained in the background. In fact, he remained so much in the background that we do not even know if he offered advice. Nevertheless, Hollywood greats, such as director John Ford and actor John Wayne, remembered meeting him. Just before his death, Wyatt was hoping that his Hollywood friends would make a movie about the O.K. Corral and the Vendetta Ride, setting the record straight, and showing him and his brothers acting honorably. He would never live to see that movie made, but in the years to come his story would be told time and again. In the process Wyatt would be transformed into a western hero.

# 9. The Legacy of Wyatt Earp

History, whether written by professional and amateur historians or created by popular culture, takes a mixed view of Wyatt Earp. During his lifetime, his adventures were exaggerated by newspapers and cheap magazines until no one could tell truth from falsehood. Wyatt made several attempts to set the record straight, but he lacked the skills of a writer or a public speaker. He was reluctant to talk about his life, and he was embarrassed by the exaggerations in the popular media. Feeling that what he had done was honorable and just, he was unable to defend himself without making it appear that the charges were true, that he was a violent and an unstable gunman. As a result, his reputation was restored only after his death, but restored, ironically, by the exaggeration of his deeds.

Wyatt's years as a policeman in Wichita and an assistant marshal in Dodge City have been celebrated by two famous television shows, neither of which had much to do with reality. The longest-running program in history, *Gunsmoke*, revolved around a beefy, sweat-stained

This is a portrait of cast members from the television show *Gunsmoke*, which ran from 1955 to 1975. James Arness as Marshal Matt Dillon stands to the left, and Amanda Blake as Kitty Russell is seated near costarring cast members. This program was supposed to be based on Wyatt's time as a lawman, though it had little to do with reality.

Marshal Dillon and his comic relief sidekicks. *The Life and Legend of Wyatt Earp* featured one of the greatest theme songs of all time, along with a dapper Wyatt Earp who apparently was too busy enforcing the law to have an interest in women and who carried a weapon that might never have existed, the Buntline Special. Both interpretations were based partly on a 1931 best-seller by Stuart Lake that portrayed Wyatt Earp in heroic terms as an honest and effective lawman whose conduct contrasted strongly with the corrupt law enforcement officials of the Depression era in 1930s America. Lake had interviewed Earp toward the end of his life, but, apparently frustrated with Wyatt's lack of story-telling skills, he relied more on his own research and imagination for the book. Moreover, Josephine had pestered him not to write anything that might not reflect well on either Wyatt or her.

Lake's version of Wyatt Earp also inspired two great Hollywood westerns, *My Darling Clementine* (1946) and *Gunfight at the O.K. Corral* (1957). Josephine's story was told in the book *I Married Wyatt Earp*. Although this best-seller was taken off the shelves by its publisher, which had concluded that the story was partly fiction, the public remained relatively unaware that the reputation of Wyatt Earp was under-going revision. Out of a cardboard cutout, historians were carving a human being who was much more com-plicated and interesting.

Recent movies have attempted to tell a more realistic Wyatt Earp story. *Tombstone* (1993) and *Wyatt Earp* (1994) were not total successes as history, though they had exciting scenes and occasional splendid acting. The problem was that the Earp story was too big to be told in two hours or even three. Still, we might well remember that Bat Masterson once said, "The real story of the Old West can never be told unless Wyatt Earp will tell what he knows, and Wyatt will not talk." Wyatt's reluctance to talk about his life and experiences left the telling to thousands of others who believed that by understanding Wyatt Earp one could understand the American West. It is the hope that we can recapture that long-lost time and make sense of the values and stories that built up the frontier that leads people back to the story of Wyatt Earp.

In trying to understand the American West, it is important to understand its values. Wyatt was not a superhero, but he was honest and straightforward. He could defend himself without being a bully, and he did not fear taking on dangerous outlaws and corrupt politicians. He made loyal friends of very interesting people. He also stood for family togetherness. In the American West, one had to rely on friends and family a great deal, because so much else was changing so fast. In practice, theories come and go. Theories reflect contemporary problems and the stresses of our own times. Stories, in contrast, tend to persist. It will probably be so

with Wyatt Earp and the story of law enforcement in the American West. Our ideas concerning Wyatt's significance will probably change over the years to come, but our fascination with the Gunfight at the O.K. Corral and the Vendetta Ride will not.

*Opposite*: In 1876, Wyatt Earp (sitting) and Bat Masterson had their photograph taken in Dodge City, where they worked together as lawmen. Neither of them was known for shooting criminals, rather they would club them over the head to knock them out and then cart them off to jail.

# Timeline

**1839**     Nicholas Earp's first wife dies. A year later he marries Virginia Ann Cooksey, Wyatt's mother.

**1845**     Nicholas and Virginia Earp move to Monmouth, Illinois.

**1847**     Nicholas Earp joins a volunteer unit called the Monmouth Dragoons and participates in the Mexican War.

**1848**     Wyatt Earp is born.

**1849–50**     The Earps move to Pella, Iowa.

**1856**     The Earps return to Monmouth.

**1859**     After being convicted and fined three times for bootlegging whiskey, Nicholas sells his property in Monmouth and moves his family to Pella, Iowa.

**1864**     Nicholas Earp leads his family on a wagon train to settle in California.

**1868**     Wyatt stops in Wyoming, where he works on the railroad, and then settles in Lamar, Missouri, to work in his father's restaurant.

| | |
|---|---|
| **1870** | Wyatt marries Rilla Sutherland. Wyatt is elected constable of Lamar. |
| **1871** | Rilla dies. Wyatt leaves Lamar and lives in Indian Territory. |
| **1874** | Wyatt takes a job as a policeman in Wichita, Kansas. |
| **1876** | Wyatt moves to Dodge City, Kansas, where he takes the job of deputy marshal. |
| **1879** | Wyatt moves to Tombstone, Arizona, where he becomes deputy sheriff. |
| **1880** | Curly Bill Brocius, leader of a cattle-rustling gang, kills Marshal Fred White. The judge rules it an accidental death. |
| **1881** | Wyatt arrests gang leader Johnny Ringo for murder, but the charges are dropped. |
| | Newton Clanton is killed in the Guadalupe Canyon Massacre. The Clanton gang blames the Earps and Doc Holliday. |
| | The Gunfight at the O.K. Corral leaves Tom and Frank McLaury and Billy Clanton dead. |
| | Virgil Earp is shot in front of a saloon, leaving his arm permanently crippled. |

**1882**    Morgan Earp is killed. Johnny Ringo is killed. The killers are never identified.

**1887**    Ike Clanton is killed.

Doc Holliday dies in bed in Colorado.

**1896**    Wyatt serves as a referee for the Sharkey–Fitzsimmons fight.

**1900**    Warren Earp is killed in a bar in Willcox, Arizona.

**1907**    Nicholas Earp dies in an old soldiers' home.

**1929**    Wyatt Earp dies in Los Angeles, California.

**1931**    Stuart Lake publishes a best-selling book based on Wyatt Earp's life.

**1946**    John Ford directs the movie *My Darling Clementine* starring Henry Fonda as Wyatt Earp.

**1955**    The television show *The Life and Legend of Wyatt Earp* debuts on ABC. The show stays on the air until 1961.

**1957**    *The Gunfight at the O.K. Corral* opens in theaters across America.

# Glossary

**ambushed** (AM-bush)  To have surprised someone with a sudden, unexpected attack.

**bootlegging** (BOOT-leg-ing)  To sell liquor illegally. Men on horseback found it easy to stash a small, thin bottle of whiskey in a boot. They could retrieve it at any time for a quick drink, and it was unlikely to spill or to break. This was also a convenient way to deliver a bottle of illegal booze to customers. The word booze has no connection to boots, but comes from Middle English bousen, to drink bad liquor.

**chaos** (KAY-ahs)  Complete disorder, with no pattern or logic in events or circumstances.

**constable** (KON-stuh-bul)  A minor court officer. In some states this was the equivalent to a policeman. In Illinois, constables were essentially process servers. City marshals formed the police force.

**cooper** (KOO-per)  A person who makes barrels or wooden tubs.

**coroner** (KOR-uh-ner)  A court official, usually a

medical doctor, who rules on the causes of unnatural deaths.

**Depression era** (dih-PREH-shun EH-ruh) The period of time in U.S. history when economic problems led to widespread unemployment and poverty, from 1929 to about 1939.

**dragoon** (druh-GOON) A military unit made up of heavily armed mounted troops.

**Emancipation Proclamation** (ih-man-sih-PAY-shun prah-kluh-MAY-shun) A document, signed by Abraham Lincoln during the Civil War, which freed all slaves held in Confederate territory.

**epitaph** (EH-puh-taf) Words carved in the stone of a tomb, in memory of the one buried there.

**expelling** (ik-SPEL-ing) Removing from a place.

**garrisons** (GAR-ih-sunz) Military posts.

**guerrillas** (guh-RIH-luz) People who engage in irregular warfare. Often part of a loosely organized group instead of an actual army.

**incriminating** (in-KRIH-muh-nayt-ing) Casting suspicion or guilt on somebody.

**indictment** (in-DYT-ment) Criminal charges brought against a suspect.

**inquest** (IN-kwest) An examination of the facts of a

case by a judge or jury.

**intrigues** (in-TREEGZ) Things that arouse the interest or the curiosity of someone.

**marshal** (MAR-shul) A U.S. marshal is a federal law officer. A city marshal enforces the law inside a town.

**pore** (POR) To study intensely.

**posse** (PAH-see) A group of men assembled by a sheriff to preserve the peace.

**prudent** (PROO-dent) Wise.

**railhead** (RAYL-hed) The station at the end of a railroad line. As railroad construction continued, many members of the community at the old railhead packed up and moved to the new end of the tracks.

**revision** (reh-VIH-zhun) To give a new and different explanation as to why something happened.

**rustled** (RUH-suhld) To have stolen cattle.

**saloon** (suh-LOON) A combination restaurant, bar, and gaming establishment. It often provided rooms for guests and private poker games.

**sheriff** (SHER-if) The chief law enforcement officer of a county.

**shunned** (SHUND) To turn one's back on someone.

**subsidy** (SUB-sih-dee) A grant or gift of money.

**testimony** (TES-tuh-moh-nee) Statements made by witnesses under oath.

**unscrupulous** (un-SKROO-pyuh-lus) Evil behavior.

**valor** (VA-lur) Bravery.

**vendetta** (ven-DEH-tuh) A bitter feud.

**vigilante** (vih-jih-LAN-tee) Having to do with loosely organized groups of private citizens who join together, usually secretly, to punish lawbreakers when the police forces or courts appear ineffective.

# Additional Resources

To learn more about Wyatt Earp, check out these books and Web sites.

## Books

Alford, Turner, ed. *The Earps Talk*. College Station, Texas: Creative Publications, 1980.

Gatto, Steve. *The Real Wyatt Earp: A Documentary Biography*. Edited by Neil B. Carmony. Silver City, New Mexico: High-Lonesome Books, 2000.

Lake, Stuart. *Wyatt Earp: Frontier Marshal*. Boston: Houghton Mifflin, 1931.

Olds, Bruce. *Bucking the Tiger*. New York: Farrar, Straus and Giroux, 2001.

## Web Sites

http://clantongang.com/oldwest/gangike.html

http://users.techline.com/nicks/earp.htm

www.tombstone-epitaph.com/

www.tombstonehistory.com/

# Bibliography

Barra, Allen. *Inventing Wyatt Earp: His Life and Many Legends*. New York: Carroll & Graf, 1998.

Shillingberg, William. *Tombstone, A.T: A History of Early Mining, Milling, and Mayhem*. Spokane, Washington: Arthur H. Clark Co., 1999.

Tefertiller, Casey. *Wyatt Earp: The Life Behind the Legend*. New York: John Wiley & Sons, 1999.

Waters, Frank. *The Earp Brothers of Tombstone. The Story of Mrs. Virgil Earp*. New York: Clarkson N. Potter, 1960.

# Index

**A**
Alamo, 61
American Revolution, 6, 17
Appalachian Mountains, 6, 9

**B**
Blaylock, Celia Ann Mattie,
    47, 53, 83
Behan, John Harris, 61, 64,
    67–69, 71–72, 75, 77, 82,
    85
Boot Hill, 49
bootleggers, 40
boxing, 86
Brocius, Curly Bill, 60, 67, 82
Buntline Special, 96

**C**
California, 21, 31, 51
cattle, 42–43, 45, 51, 60–61,
    69, 71
Civil War, 28, 30, 35, 45
Claiborne, Billy, 75, 77
clan, 15
Clanton, Billy, 67, 75, 77
Clanton, Ike, 71–74, 77–78,
    80–81, 85
Clanton, Newton, 71
County Ring, 61
cowboy(s), 42–43, 45, 49,
    60–61, 65–69, 71–75, 77,
    79–80, 82, 85

**D**
Dodge City, Kansas, 42, 49, 52,
    94

**E**
Earp, Allie, 80
Earp, Virgil, 28, 33, 52–54, 64,
    67–69, 71–75, 77, 80, 85,
    89
Earp, Warren, 71, 80
Earp, Walter, 9–10, 15, 23
Earp, Wyatt
    birth, 21
    death, 90
    father, 10, 14–15, 17,
        21–23, 26, 31, 33, 35,
        51–52, 89
    mother, 14
Elder, Kate, 53, 69
Emancipation Proclamation,
    40

**F**
Frémont, John Charles, 22, 53,
    67

**G**
Gadsen Purchase, 51–52
Guadalupe Canyon Massacre,
    71
gunfight(s), 50, 65, 78
*Gunsmoke*, 94

**H**
Hart, Willliam S., 90
Holliday, John Henry "Doc",
    49–50, 53, 66–69, 71–72,
    75, 80, 83, 85
Hollywood, California, 90, 93,
    96

**I**
Indian Territory, 35, 38, 40, 42

**L**
Lamar, Missouri, 33, 35, 43

Lincoln, Abraham, 26

**M**
Marcus, Josephine Sarah, 61,
    64, 78, 86, 96
Masterson, William Barclay
    "Bat", 38, 68, 83, 97
McLaury, Frank, 75, 77
McLaury, Tom, 72–73, 77
Mexican War, 17, 21
Mix, Tom, 90
Monmouth, Illinois, 14–15, 17,
    21–23, 26
Monmouth Dragoons, 19

**N**
Native American(s), 9, 31, 38,
    40

**O**
Oregon Trail, 31, 51

**P**
Pella, Iowa, 21, 26
Pioneer Cemetery, 14

**R**
Ringo, Johnny, 60, 68, 85

**S**
Santa Fe Trail, 52
settler(s), 6, 8–11, 31
Sharkey-Fitzsimmons fight,
    86–87
Sierra Nevada, 31
Stillwell, Frank, 71, 81
Sutherland, Rilla, 35, 47

**T**
tall tales, 30
Texas Rangers, 19

Tombstone, Arizona, 13, 50,
    52, 54, 57–58, 60–61, 64,
    66–69, 71–72, 85
tuberculosis, 50, 85

**U**
U.S. marshal(s), 38, 54, 58, 64,
    71, 82

**V**
Vendetta Ride, 82, 89, 93
vigilante(s), 71, 82

**W**
War of 1812, 6, 17
Wayne, John, 93
Wells Fargo, 55, 73

# About the Author

William Urban is the Lee L. Morgan professor of history at Monmouth College in Monmouth, Illinois. He has published several articles on Wyatt Earp's family. One of these, "The People versus Nicholas P. Earp," won the Harry E. Pratt Memorial Award for the best article published in the *Illinois Historical Journal* during the year 1997. He has also published more than a dozen books and was editor of the *Journal of Baltic Studies* from 1990 to 1994. He grew up in Oklahoma and Kansas, and as a boy heard his grandmothers tell stories of their parents' adventures and hardships on the Great Plains in pioneer days. One of his grandmothers was actually born in a sod house on the prairie.

# Credits

## Photo Credits

Cover: courtesy the Craig Fouts Collection (main photo); courtesy Arizona Historical Society/Tucson (background photo); p. 4 courtesy the Craig Fouts Collection; p. 7 courtesy of Map Division, the New York Public Library, Astor, Lenox and Tilden Foundations; p. 8 Record Group 11, General Records of the U.S. Government, National Archives and Records Administration, Old Military and Civil Records; p. 9 courtesy Washington University Gallery of Art, St. Louis, Missouri, gift of Nathaniel Philips; pp. 16, 84 © Daguerreotype Collection, Library of Congress Prints and Photographs Division, Washington, D.C. 20540 USA; pp. 18, 20, 27 © Library of Congress Prints and Photographs Division, Washington, D.C. 20540 USA; pp. 19, 48, 60, 61, 78, 81, 98 courtesy Arizona Historical Society/Tucson; p. 23 © David J. & Francis L. Frent Collection/CORBIS; pp. 24-25 © Library of Congress Geography and Map Division, Washington, D.C., G4104.M7A3 1869 .R8 Rug 25; pp. 28, 44, 95 ©Bettmann/CORBIS; p. 32 courtesy Denver Public Library Western History Department; p. 36 © Library of Congress Rare Book & Special Collections Division; p. 38 Collection of R.G. McCubbin; p. 47 Kansas State Historical Society; p. 49 Western History Collections, University of Oklahoma Libraries; p. 51 Camilius S. Fly, Arizona Historical Society/Tucson; p. 54 courtesy George Stumpf, Deputy U.S. Marshal, (Ret); p. 55 © Library of Congress, Prints and Photographs Division, Washington, D.C. 20540 USA, Historic American Buildings Survey or Historic American Engineering Record, HABS,UTAH,27-SILV,1-2; pp. 59, 79 courtesy *Tombstone Epitaph*, Tombstone, AZ, 85638; p. 62 © Lowell Georgia/CORBIS; p. 63 photograph by Camilius S. Fly, Tombstone, AZ, courtesy of Stephen and Marge Elliott, Tombstone Western Heritage Museum; p. 64 Donald C. & Elizabeth M. Dickinson Research Center, National Cowboy & Western Heritage Museum; p. 66 © Dover Pictorial Archive Series; p. 70 Camilius S. Fly , © collection of the New-York Historical Society NYHS # 40746; p. 72 Hassell © collection of the New-York Historical Society NYHS# 40747; p. 74 photograph By Camilius S. Fly, Tombstone, AZ, courtesy of Stephen and Marge Elliott, Tombstone Western Heritage Museum, From the collection of the daughter of Dr. George Goodfellow, prominent Tombstone surgeon who treated Virgil Earp for shotgun wounds received at the hands of the Clanton gang; p. 76 courtesy of the Autry Museum of Western Heritage; p. 83 © Mark Gibson/CORBIS; p. 84 National Museum of American History (S.I.), Division of Science, Medicine, and Society; pp. 87, 92 courtesy of Stephen and Marge Elliott, Tombstone Western Heritage Museum; p. 90 photo by Dick George

**Editors** Jason Moring and Joanne Randolph

**Series Design** Laura Murawski

**Layout Design** Corinne Jacob

**Photo Researcher** Jeffrey Wendt